Recommended

Country
Hotels

OF BRITAIN

1993

INCLUDING COUNTRY
HOUSE HOLIDAYS

FHG PUBLICATIONS, Paisley

Our 'Cover' Hotels

⬆ MILLWATERS, Newbury Berkshire
For further information about our Front Cover featured hotel,
see the full description under Berkshire.

⬆ THE STEPPES, near Hereford, Herefordshire
As well as the Outside Back Cover, see the full description in
the Herefordshire section.

The Old Mill Hotel & Restaurant

Tollbridge Road, Bath, Avon BA1 7DE
Telephone: (0225) 858476

Visit the beautiful Georgian city with Roman Baths!

Only 15 minutes from the M4 Junction 17 or 18

Only 5 minutes from City Centre

RAC** ETB 👑👑👑

*Enjoy the picturesque setting of this **Riverside** hotel on the banks of the Avon, beside historic Toll Bridge overlooking the Weir and breathtaking panoramic views. **Turn with the Wheel** in the **unique Revolving Waterwheel Restaurant** – the base gently turns with 23ft waterwheel showing varied river views.*

* Luxurious ensuite bedrooms mostly with river views, colour TV, telephone, etc. * <u>Honeymooners' Paradise</u> – celebrate those special occasions in romantic, four-poster river view bedrooms!
Special welcoming packs!

* Riverside Bar * Sunday Lunches * Wedding Receptions and Parties * Fishing * Car Park

Mid week – Singles *from* £35; Doubles from £25 per person.
Weekends – Singles *from* £40; Doubles from £26.50 per person.
Enquire for Short Break discounts & Family Rooms.

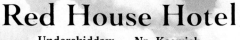

GREAT TREE HOTEL

Sandy Park, Near Chagford,
Devon TQ13 8JS
Telephone: Chagford (0647) 432491
Telex: 9312132116 (GT G)
Telecom Gold Mail Box 72; MAG 37130

An idyllic situation, quiet and very secluded situated as it is in 18 acres of its own gardens and woods in the Dartmoor foothills. There are splendid views from the spacious lounge with its beams, beautifully carved oak stairway and log fire. (No problem with logs here.) A cosy bar and a small intimate dining room serviced by chefs with a leaning towards traditional menus and who obtain much of their ingredients straight from the hotel's own gardens or from local farmers. Most of the rooms are on the ground floor, face south, and enjoy magnificent views over the gardens and the surrounding countryside. All are comfortably furnished with private bathrooms, colour television, tea and coffee making facilities and private telephones.
A homely and friendly atmosphere, a delightful place to unwind.

Contact: Beverley and Nigel Eaton-Gray

Where Dorset meets Devon

Peace and Tranquillity

Welcoming Country House, with 20 luxury ensuite bedrooms, award winning gardens, views across the Axe Valley and near the coast at Lyme Regis.

FAIRWATER HEAD COUNTRY HOUSE HOTEL
Hawkchurch (the village of Roses), Devon, EX13 5TX
Telephone: (0297) 678349

**AA ★★★ RAC Awards for Hospitality, Restaurant, Comfort
Egon Ronay, BTA Commended, Ashley Courtenay**

H·I·G·H·B·U·L·L·E·N

CHITTLEHAMHOLT, UMBERLEIGH, N. DEVON EX37 9HD
Telephone: (0769) 540561   Fax: (0769) 540492

Chittlehamholt lies in the heart of the Devon countryside, south of Exmoor and only a short drive from the coast and beaches.

Highbullen, a splendid Victorian Gothic mansion stands on high ground in sixty acres of parkland, with fine views over the surrounding countryside. Life here is informal with many quiet hideaways.

The extensive cellars are now the social and gastronomic heart of the hotel. The restaurant serving an excellent 'table d'hote' dinner with wide choice, has appeared in all the reputable guides for over 25 years.

All bedrooms have private bathroom, colour T.V. and direct dial telephone. Many are situated in the Home Farm and converted cottages within the grounds. INDOOR and outdoor tennis, UNLIMITED FREE GOLF on the 9 hole par 31 course (professional's shop). Squash, croquet and billiards. Massage and hairdressing by arrangement. Indoor and outdoor swimming pools, sauna and steam-room, spa-bath, sunbed and indoor putting green.

KEMPS
COUNTRY HOUSE
& HOTEL
RESTAURANT

East Stoke, Wareham,
Dorset BH20 6AL
Telephone: Bindon Abbey
(0929) 462563
Fax: (0929) 405287

Originally built as a Victorian rectory, Kemps is situated in its own grounds rising from the valley of the River Frome, with lovely views of the Purbeck Hills.

The Victorian atmosphere is faithfully preserved and the spacious new bedrooms are pristine and tastefully decorated. There is a 4 poster bed in the honeymoon suite and some bedrooms have whirlpool baths.

The attractive dining room has been enhanced with the addition of a Victorian conservatory extension which overlooks the garden and hills.

Kemps Restaurant is Egon Ronay recommended and is well known for imaginative cooking using fresh produce and fresh bread is baked daily.

ALL YEAR BARGAIN BREAKS   ETB 👑👑👑👑 Commended

O L D C O U R T
Newent, Gloucestershire. Proprietors: Ron and Sue Wood

The Old Court is a magnificent William and Mary house set in its own mature, walled gardens of over an acre. The old market town of Newent is close to the Wye Valley, the Cotswolds and the Forest of Dean. All bedrooms are large and comfortable having colour TV and tea and coffee making facilities. Several rooms are ensuite. Restaurant licence. An interesting range of traditional and continental cuisine is served in the popular restaurant using much local produce with a wide selection of fine wines. Several golf courses are nearby, as well as the famous Falconry Centre, Vineyards, Butterfly Centre, National Waterways Museum and many other places of interest to visit.

From £29.50 per person per night, Dinner, Bed and Breakfast.
Short Breaks available for couples from £84.00 per couple for two nights.
Telephone: Newent (0531) 820522

String of Horses

**Mead End, Sway
Lymington
Hampshire
SO41 6EH
Tel: 0590 682631**

Unique secluded, exclusive hotel set in four acres in the heart of the New Forest, with a friendly relaxed atmosphere. Eight luxurious double bedrooms are available, each with its own fantasy bathroom with spa bath and shower. Every facility is offered including colour television, direct-dial telephone, radio and tea-making facilities. Four-poster rooms are also available, making this an ideal honeymoon setting. Dine in our intimate candlelit "Carriages" restaurant. For relaxation there is a heated outdoor swimming pool. This is superb riding country, and the hotel is close to excellent yachting resorts and several good golf courses.

ETB ♕ ♕ ♕ ♕ **Highly Commended   AA** Rosette**

RATES: *Inclusive of*
FULL ENGLISH BREAKFAST of:
Freshly Laid Eggs, Bacon Rashers,
Local Mushrooms, Tomatoes and
Traditional Sausages

DOUBLES from £39.50 per person
per night

SUITES (*with exceptionally spacious
sitting rooms*) from £59.50 per person
per night

Book 4 nights stay **one extra** night **free**
5 nights stay **two extra** nights **free**

A luxury Georgian country house hotel set in four acres of grounds opening onto the beautiful New Forest. The Woodlands Lodge Hotel is a newly re-opened **luxury hotel** offering peace and tranquillity often only found in buildings of age and establishment. The **interior decor** is quite stunning with all bedrooms individually designed.

All eighteen bedrooms and suites enjoy **full en-suite facilities** of Jacuzzi Bath, separate Thermastic Shower with some bathrooms also having bidets. The **sumptuous** kingsize pocket sprung beds are possibly the most comfortable beds guests have slept on (this opinion is constantly being expressed by guests). All other amenities are present including 21" FastText T.V., Writing Desks, Armchairs, Hairdryer, Trouser Press, Teasmaid, Telephone.

At **Woodlands Lodge** the hotel service is very friendly and informal thus enabling guests to relax totally and feel at home. Our dinner menu is modestly priced at a maximum of £16.95 (including à la carte) for three courses and coffee-something for absolutely everyone!! Our modestly priced wine list with Piesporter Michelberg at £6.95 a bottle to Chateauneuf du Pape at £10.50 a bottle must offer excellent value for money. **Please come and spoil yourself.**

THE WOODLANDS LODGE HOTEL
BARTLEY ROAD, WOODLANDS, NEW FOREST SO4 2GN

AA ★★★   RESERVATIONS 0703 292257   E.T.B. ♕♕♕♕ HIGHLY COMMENDED

Please mention
Recommended COUNTRY HOTELS
when seeking refreshment or
accommodation at a Hotel
mentioned in these pages

DALE HILL GOLF HOTEL

TICEHURST, WADHURST, EAST SUSSEX TN5 7DQ

The warmest of welcomes awaits you at one of England's finest new hotels, set in 300 acres of outstanding natural beauty. A small luxury leisure centre with indoor swimming pool, full beauty and massage treatments, together with a superb 18 hole established parkland golf course and award winning restaurant, all add up to the luxury you deserve.

AA/RAC ★★★★
⊛ Restaurant
English Tourist Board
♛♛♛♛♛
Highly Commended
Michelin
Tel: 0580 200112

The Lodge

English Tourist Board
HIGHLY COMMENDED
♛♛♛♛

COUNTRY HOUSE HOTEL

Middleton Road, Pickering,
North Yorkshire YO18 8NQ
Telephone: (0751) 72976

A peaceful country house hotel secluded amidst three acres of lawns and terraces, The Lodge offers superb accommodation throughout. The delightful guest rooms are all en suite, with direct-dial telephone, hospitality trays and colour television. A charming bar and gracious drawing room both overlook the gardens. Whilst a lovely Victorian conservatory restaurant provides the perfect setting to enjoy a delicious selection of traditional and more adventurous cuisine, all prepared and presented to the highest possible standards. Fully licensed. This delightful hotel is situated on the outskirts of Pickering, the natural centre from which to explore the North Yorkshire Moors, the Heritage Coast and historic York.

WOOD HALL

Trip Lane, Linton, Near Wetherby, West Yorkshire LS22 4JA
Tel: (0937) 587271 Fax: (0937) 584353

ETB 👑👑👑👑👑
DELUXE
1992 Egon Ronay 80%   RAC ★★★★
                       AA ★★★

The approach to Wood Hall through carefully tended parkland, over a stone bridge and then onto a wide sweep of terrace fills one with a sense of pleasurable anticipation. One's immediate reaction on catching sight of this fine house is complete satisfaction, because here a Georgian mansion has been sensitively refurbished to create a country house hotel of unique charm and character. The 44 bedrooms are of luxurious standard, and for that extra special occasion, suites with private sitting rooms and magnificent four-poster beds are available. Sumptuous soft furnishings, oak panelling and elegant decor in the public rooms, combined with attentive but unobtrusive service, put the final gloss on the excellent reputation Wood Hall has gained far beyond the borders of Yorkshire.

PLEASE NOTE

*There is a full description of each of our
Colour Section advertisers . . .*

*. . . in the appropriate County Section of
RECOMMENDED COUNTRY HOTELS
as detailed on our Contents Page.*

ARDSTINCHAR HOTEL

Main Street · Ballantrae · Near Girvan KA26 0NB ☎ (046-583) 254

Renowned for personal, friendly service and excellent food. The hotel is situated in a picturesque small village with bowling and putting greens. Close to sea with magnificent views and ideal for hill walking. Five major golf courses in the area. Golf and fishing can be arranged, as can pottery classes. Horse riding and bird sanctuary nearby. All rooms have showers and washbasins. Bed and Breakfast from £15; with Evening Meal from £23. Reductions for children.

Spean Bridge, near Fort William, Inverness-shire PH34 4EU

Telephone: 039-781 335

2 Crowns Approved

DRUIMANDARROCH HOUSE

Druimandarroch House is a small, personally run hotel which stays small to ensure you get personal service. We are ideally situated for carefree days of touring, coming back to dinner or a basket meal and a drink. All rooms have colour TV and tea/coffee making equipment and two rooms have private facilities. Children and pets welcome. There is a golf course nearby.

Inflation Beaters – 1991 prices throughout 1993 at Druimandarroch. We look forward to welcoming you.

Linndhu Country House Hotel

Tobermory
Isle of Mull

Telephone
(0688) 2425

Jennifer and Ian McLean offer you a warm welcome at Linndhu. Set in 35 acres of woodland and beautiful gardens, with magnificent views over the Sound of Mull, this traditional Highland hotel brings you superb comfort and imaginative, delicious cuisine. A trout stream flows through the grounds, and we can arrange river, loch and sea fishing. Maybe you'll want to walk, golf, birdwatch, deerstalk, or just relax and enjoy the island's spectacular scenery – the choice is yours. We are just 2 miles south of Tobermory on the A848 Salen to Tobermory road.

KEPPOCH HOUSE HOTEL

APPROVED

Perth Road, Crieff PH7 3EQ
Tel: (0764) 4341
Fax: (0764) 5435

This charming hotel is located on the Perth road only 10 minutes' walk from the centre of Crieff. Situated within its own grounds and having a southerly aspect, its location offers beautiful views of the Vale of Strathearn and the imposing Ochil Hills. After an enjoyable day at one of the many golf courses or fishing rivers or lochs in this area, relax in comfortable surroundings and enjoy a delicious evening meal cooked from local, fresh produce.
Further details from Mr Bob Brown.

Craigower Hotel

134 Atholl Road, Pitlochry PH16 5AB
Telephone: Management & Booking (0796) 472590
Guests   (0796) 472351
Facsimile   (0796) 472590

Craigower is family run hotel in the centre of Pitlochry. We offer 26 comfortable en-suite bedrooms with TV, hospitality tray, direct-dial telephone and hairdryers. There is weekly entertainment in the hotel and arrangements can be made for booking tickets at the world-famous "Theatre in the Hills". Golf can be arranged at one of the many local courses, as can fishing and shooting.
Freshly prepared meals served, using local produce.

Recommended
COUNTRY HOTELS
OF BRITAIN 1993

WITH FACILITIES improving and prices either falling or holding steady, these are times which favour visitors to most hotels in Britain. Perhaps many of our best country hotels may have survived the last year or two more successfully than others because they had already established a reputation for high standards and good value for money. Those hotels which are slow to learn the lesson of rising consumer expectation cannot hope to remain afloat for long, let alone flourish in an age of competition and increased leisure time.

In this 1993 edition of RECOMMENDED COUNTRY HOTELS OF BRITAIN we have tried to improve our service to you, our readers, by offering for the first time, a small selection of entries illustrated in full colour. You will find these hotels also represented, often more fully, in our classified county sections which contain many old favourites, fully revised and updated, as well as new prospects for you to explore. As usual, therefore, our main aim remains to give you a wide choice of hotels of character and quality for your holiday and/or business travel accommodation.

In addition to information about location, accommodation, cuisine and cellar, with most entries we also give an indication of price range and of course whatever ratings or awards individual hotels may have achieved. Our hotels are 'recommended' for their reputation, facilities and in many cases, through long association rather than by inspection. As publishers we cannot accept responsibility for any errors or misrepresentations in the descriptions that follow and we are always interested to hear from our readers about their own experiences. Problems are best settled in the spot with the hotel itself but we will record any complaint we receive and follow it up. We regret, however, that we cannot act as intermediaries or arbiters.

In the many years since the first edition of RECOMMENDED COUNTRY HOTELS was published, complaints have been few, and rarely serious. You will find straightforward and mainly factual descriptions of a selection of many old favourites and newer entries. As far as we can establish, all details are correct as we go to press, but we suggest that you confirm prices and any other terms when you enquire about bookings.

We would be grateful if you mention RECOMMENDED COUNTRY HOTELS when you enquire or book. We will be more than happy to receive your recommendations (in preference, hopefully to problems, as mentioned above!) and in particular of any hotels which you may judge worthy of inclusion.

Peter Stanley Williams
Editorial Consultant

Peter Clark
Publishing Director

Recommended
Country Hotels
OF BRITAIN

CONTENTS

Other FHG Publications 1993

Recommended Wayside Inns of Britain
Recommended Short-Break Holidays in Britain
Pets Welcome!
Bed and Breakfast in Britain
The Golf Guide: Where to Play/Where to Stay
Farm Holiday Guide England/Wales
Farm Holiday Guide Scotland
Self-Catering & Furnished Holidays
Britain's Best Holidays
Guide to Caravan and Camping Holidays
Bed and Breakfast Stops
Children Welcome! Family Holiday Guide

We thank the Millwaters Hotel & Restaurant of Newbury
for the use of their picture on our Outside Front Cover.

Cover design: Edward Carden (Glasgow)

1993 Edition
ISBN 1 85055 160 X
© FHG Publications Ltd.
No part of this publication may be reproduced by any means or
transmitted without the permission of the Publishers.

Cartography by GEO Projects, Reading
Maps are based on Ordnance Survey maps with the permission of
the Controller of Her Majesty's Stationery Office. Crown copyright reserved.

Typeset by RD Composition Ltd., Glasgow.
Printed and bound in Great Britain by Richard Clay & Co., Bungay, Suffolk.
Distribution. **Book Trade:** WLM, 117 The Hollow, Littleover, Derby DE3 7BS
(Tel: 0332 272020. Fax: 0332 774287).
News Trade: UMD, 1 Benwell Road, Holloway, London N7 7AX (Tel: 071-700 4600. Fax: 071-607 3352).

Published by FHG Publications Ltd.
Abbey Mill Business Centre, Seedhill, Paisley PA1 1TJ (041-887 0428).
A member of the U.N. Group.

US ISBN 1-55650-546-9
Distributed in the United States by
Hunter Publishing Inc., 300 Raritan Center Parkway, CN94,
Edison, N.J., 08818, USA

Avon

THE BATH TASBURGH HOTEL,
Warminster Road, Bathampton,
Bath, Avon BA2 6SH

Tel: 0225 425096/463842
Fax: 0225 425096

Residential licence; 12 bedrooms, 11 with private bathrooms; Historic interest; Children welcome; Car park (15); City centre one mile; ££.

This family-owned Victorian country house, built for a photographer to the Royal family, is set in seven acres of lovely gardens and grounds, with canal frontage and magnificent views across the Avon valley. Extensively refurbished, the house retains many original features, and offers tastefully furnished rooms with all the modern comforts of a good hotel — en suite bath/shower, direct-dial telephone, radio, colour television and tea/coffee facilities in all rooms. Four-poster and ground floor rooms available. There are fine breakfast and sitting rooms and a conservatory for guests. One of the important features is the personal care and attention given by Brian and Audrey Archer, creating a country house atmosphere so near and convenient to Bath city centre. *ETB Highly Commended, AA, RAC Highly Acclaimed, Les Routiers.* **See also Colour Advertisement p.4.**

The **£** symbol when appearing at the end of the italic section of an entry shows the anticipated price, during 1993, for a **single room with English Breakfast.**

Under £30	**£**	**Over £45 but under £60**	**£££**
Over £30 but under £45	**££**	**Over £60**	**££££**

This is meant as an indication only and does not show prices for Special Breaks, Weekends, etc. Guests are therefore advised to verify all prices on enquiring or booking.

THE OLD MILL HOTEL AND RESTAURANT,
Tollbridge Road, Bath,
Avon BA1 7DE

Tel: 0225 858746
Fax: 0225 852600

Licensed; 15 bedrooms, all with private bathrooms; Historic interest; Children welcome; Car park (35); Bristol 13 miles; ££.

What could be more luxurious than enjoying yourself in the relaxed and picturesque setting of the Old Mill Hotel, set on the banks of the River Avon, by the historic Toll Bridge and with fishing facilities? The hotel offers superb accommodation, most of the en suite bedrooms having breathtaking views of the river. All rooms have colour television and telephone, and some have four-poster beds. Delicious meals can be enjoyed in the à la carte restaurant, the floor of which is gently rotated by the waterwheel, giving diners varied riverside views. There is a fully licensed bar where bar meals and business lunches are available. This unique hotel is only two miles from the city centre. **See Full Page Colour Advertisement p.3.** *ETB* 🏵 🏵 🏵, *RAC**.*

THE OLD SCHOOL HOUSE,
Church Street, Bathford, Bath,
Avon BA1 7RR

Tel: 0225 859593

Residential licence; 4 bedrooms, all with en suite bathrooms; Historic interest; Car park (6); Salisbury 35 miles, Bristol 13, Bath 3; ££.

This charming Victorian stone building situated in the conservation area of Bathford village enjoys lovely views over the beautiful Avon Valley and Avon Trust Nature Reserve, and is an excellent walking and touring centre. After 140 years as the village school, the Old School House now offers comfortable accommodation and friendly personal service in the informal atmosphere of a country home, with winter log fires and candlelit dinners. There are four double/twin bedrooms, each with central heating, double glazing, en suite bathrooms, tea/coffee and hairdrying facilities, colour television and telephone. There are two ground floor rooms for the less mobile. Terms: £59-£64 double. Period reductions and Winter Breaks: details available on application. **The Old School is a no smoking house.** *ETB* 🏵 🏵 🏵 *Highly Commended, AA QQQQ Selected, RAC Highly Acclaimed.*

REDWOOD LODGE HOTEL AND COUNTRY CLUB,
Beggar Bush Lane, Failand, Bristol,
Avon BS8 3TG

Tel: 0275 393901
Fax: 0275 392104

Fully licensed; 108 bedrooms, all with private bathrooms; Children welcome, guide dogs only;
Car park; M5 3 miles; ££££.

The choice of superb leisure facilities at this conveniently placed hotel is almost bewildering. There are badminton, squash and floodlit tennis courts, saunas, solaria and a fitness studio and indoor, outdoor and children's pools. What is more, the latest film releases may be viewed in the hotel's own cinema. Secluded, yet only 10 minutes from Bristol, Redwood Lodge is of great appeal to the actively inclined and is also an ideal touring base, whilst the Clifton Suspension Bridge and Avon Gorge are just a mile away. Despite its somewhat severe architectural style, the accommodation lacks nothing in the way of sophisticated appointments and the cuisine is highly regarded.

Berkshire

MILLWATERS HOTEL,
London Road, Newbury,
Berkshire RG13 2BY

Tel: 0635 528838
Fax: 0635 523406

Licensed; 32 bedrooms, all with private bathrooms; Historic interest; Children and pets
welcome; Car park (50); London 54 miles, Oxford 26; ££££.

Idyllic, romantic — these are only two of the epithets that describe, somewhat inadequately, the beautiful 8 acre gardens of Millwaters. The Rivers Kennet and Lambourn meander quietly past tree-fringed lawns where one may play croquet or boules: peace and utter contentment induced by nature's beauty. Contributing equally, in a practical sense, to this happy mood are the magnificent amenities provided at this lovely 18th century hotel. Dining sumptuously in the gorgeous Oasis Restaurant is the ultimate eating experience, fine food enhanced by charming service. Millwaters is a wonderful weekend retreat: from fishing to photography, special interest breaks may be combined with splendid relaxation. And as a touring centre, this delightfully furnished hotel is only an hour's drive from Stratford-on-Avon, the Cotswolds, Bath, Oxford, Windsor, London and the coast, whilst a day at the races at nearby Newbury or Ascot is an attractive proposition. The accommodation is superb, each guest's room a virtual suite with its own individual decor. Each has a sitting area with river, garden or courtyard view and many also have a balcony or patio; all have a private bathroom with shower and bath, radio alarm, tea and coffee-making facilities and many thoughtful extras. Heartily recommended in all aspects of guest care, Millwaters is a justly popular venue for conferences, weddings and other social functions for which arrangements are of the highest order.
👑 👑 👑 👑 👑, *AA and RAC***, Egon Ronay, Ashley Courtenay.*

OAKLEY COURT HOTEL,
Windsor Road, Water Oakley, Windsor, Berkshire SL4 5UR

Tel: 0628 74141
Fax: 0628 37011

Fully licensed; 92 bedrooms, all with private bathrooms; Historic interest; Children welcome; Car park (120); Windsor 3 miles; ££££.

Oakley Court is a magnificent country house on the banks of the River Thames, just three miles from Royal Windsor. The accommodation is superb and boating opportunities equally so. Embarking from the hotel's own jetty, one may choose from a range of vessels to suit the occasion from a launch with capacity for 100 guests to a chauffeured punt for two. All bedrooms and suites have bathroom and shower en suite, remote control colour television, direct-dial telephone and a host of extras. The imaginative cuisine, in the care of one of England's leading chefs, is known far and wide for its excellence. The grand house stands in 35 acres of lovely landscaped grounds which incorporate a 9-hole Par 3 golf course and croquet lawn and there are exclusive fishing rights on the river. 🐦🐦🐦🐦🐦 *De Luxe, AA Two Rosettes, Egon Ronay.*

Buckinghamshire

DANESFIELD HOUSE HOTEL,
Medmenham, Marlow, Buckinghamshire SL7 3ES

Tel: 0628 891010
Fax: 0628 890408

Fully licensed; 93 bedrooms, all with private bathrooms; Historic interest; Children welcome, guide dogs only; Car park (150); Marlow 3 miles; ££££.

Designed and built in sumptuous style towards the end of the 19th century and subsequently subject to neglect and decline, Danesfield House rose like a Phoenix from the ashes, opening on 1st July 1991 as a superbly appointed hotel set in 65 acres of magnificent grounds and formal gardens overlooking the River Thames between Marlow and Henley. This far-sighted and skilled undertaking has provided luxurious suites and bedrooms equipped with the finest modern amenities available, whilst there are no less than four splendid restaurants serving choice English, Italian, French and seafood cuisine. Comfortable elegance typifies the grand public rooms of this imposing and impressive house which also has wonderful facilities for banquets and other functions. 🐦🐦🐦🐦🐦, ****.

Cambridgeshire

GARDEN HOUSE HOTEL,
Granta Place, Mill Lane, Cambridge, Cambridgeshire CB2 1RT

Tel: 0223 63421
Fax: 0223 316605

Fully licensed; 118 bedrooms, all with private bathrooms; Children welcome; Car park (180); London 55 miles; ££££.

In three acres of secluded and tranquil gardens overlooking the River Cam, it is hard to believe that this splendid modern hotel is only within strolling distance of the city centre and a mere three miles from the M11. Elegant and beautifully appointed, this is a wonderful place in which to stay whilst exploring the historic and architectural joys of Cambridge. Furthermore, its facilities for conferences and social functions are amongst the very best in the country with an expert and co-operative staff to arrange every detail. Guest rooms are superbly decorated and appointed, each having a private bathroom, direct-dial telephone, trouser press, television with Sky channels, mini-bar, tea and coffee-making facilities and much more besides to ensure the ultimate in practical comforts. One of the experiences not to be missed is dining in the spacious Le Jardin Restaurant with its lovely views of garden and river. Both table d'hôte and à la carte menus offer an imaginative and mouth-watering selection of dishes, all delightfully presented. Our own choice from the à la carte menu, for hors d'oeuvres — Salade de Poitrine d'Oie et Venaison Fumée (slices of smoked goose breast and smoked venison fillet with a sharp orange dressing) followed by Etuvée de Homard Cardinal (lobster cooked in brandy and bound in a cream and tomato sauce glazed in the shell with breadcrumbs). One hopes self-imposed restraint will allow room for, perhaps, Bananes Flambées (bananas cooked with sultanas, brown sugar, dark rum and cream). 🏵 🏵 🏵 🏵, AA and RAC ****.

OLD BRIDGE HOTEL,
Huntingdon,
Cambridgeshire PE18 6TQ

Tel: 0480 52681
Fax: 0480 411017

Fully licensed; 26 bedrooms, all with private bathrooms; Historic interest; Children and pets welcome; Car park (50); Cambridge 16 miles; ££££.

A handsome creeper-clad 18th century building, this delightfully decorated hotel overlooks the River Ouse. Popular with regular visitors as well as the locals of this charming and historic town, the hotel boasts a restaurant that is famed far and wide for the flair with which its traditional dishes are presented. An extensive cold buffet may be enjoyed whilst studying the attractive murals on the terrace at lunchtime and the wine list is remarkable for its scope and quality. Furnished throughout in sympathy with its original character, the panelled dining room and main lounge feature fine fabrics and quality prints and guest rooms are blessed with the best modern amenities including satellite television. The hotel also has superb conference and function facilities. *AA *** and Rosette, Egon Ronay.*

Cheshire

CRAXTON WOOD HOTEL,
Parkgate Road, Puddington,
Cheshire L66 9PB

Tel: 051-339 4717*
Fax: 051-339 1740

Restaurant and residential licence; 14 bedrooms, all with private bathrooms; Children welcome; Car park (40); Chester 7 miles; ££££.

Basking resplendent amidst woods, lawns and rose beds which form the lovely grounds, this impressive house is located in the heart of pastoral Wirral yet within easy reach of Liverpool, Manchester and historic Chester. Apart from providing guests with the ultimate in comfort, great emphasis is placed on the ability to present a cuisine worth travelling many miles to enjoy. In attendance is a remarkable selection of wines to grace any palate. After dining, a stroll by the floodlit stream in the grounds will contribute to a feeling of ease and tranquillity, a mood completed by repose in a superbly-appointed bedroom with bathroom en suite. *AA Rosette, Egon Ronay.*

Cornwall

TREDETHY COUNTRY HOTEL,
Helland Bridge, Bodmin,
Cornwall PL30 4QS

Tel: 020-884 262/364
Fax: 020-884 707

Residential and restaurant licence; 11 bedrooms, all with private bathrooms; Historic interest; Children welcome; Car park (30); Bodmin 3 miles; ££.

Equidistant from Cornwall's north and south coasts, this delightful retreat basks in 9 acres of glorious grounds, a haven of peace and contentment. Through the lush valley in which Tredethy stands, the River Camel meanders its way to Padstow and the sea. In these idyllic surroundings, there are opportunities for riding, walking, sailing, golf and both river and sea fishing; in the grounds is a fine, sheltered, heated swimming pool. The accommodation is spacious and of a high standard, guest rooms of various sizes all having en suite facilities, colour television and telephone. Also, in the grounds, are several self-catering cottages. All arrangements are under the personal supervision of Proprietors, Beryl and Richard Graham. *WCTB* ♣ ♣ ♣.

WILLAPARK MANOR HOTEL,
Bossiney, Near Tintagel,
Cornwall PL34 0BA

Tel: 0840 770782

Restaurant and residential licence; 14 bedrooms, all with private bathrooms; Children and pets welcome; Camelford 4 miles; £.

ONE OF THE MOST BEAUTIFULLY SITUATED HOTELS IN ENGLAND. Beautiful character house, perched on the cliffs amidst 14 acres of landscaped gardens and secluded woodland overlooking the Bay. Direct access to coast path and beach with wonderful walks in every direction. 14 bedrooms, all en suite, with colour television and tea makers. Excellent cuisine, well stocked cocktail bar and a unique friendly and informal atmosphere. *ETB* ♣ ♣ ♣.

Small sailing boats line up on the pebble beach at Clovelly, one of the exceptionally pretty cliff villages of Cornwall. A single street of steps descends from the clifftop and no wheeled traffic is permitted, cars being parked above the village.

NARE HOTEL,
Carne Beach, Veryan, Truro, Cornwall TR2 5PF

Tel: 0872 501279*
Fax: 0872 501856

Restaurant and residential licence; 36 bedrooms, all with private bathrooms; Historic interest; Children and pets welcome; Car park (80); Mevagissey 7 miles; ££££.

Exuding traditional country house charm, this superbly appointed hotel will appeal to guests seeking tranquillity and the ultimate in comfort and service. Surrounded by National Trust land, the hotel stands in solitary splendour, its extensive grounds having breathtaking views over Gerrans Bay and the lovely Roseland Peninsula. In company with the pervading air of elegance are rooms furnished with antiques and fresh flowers, adding piquancy to the tasteful decor. Log fires and central heating combat the onset of cooler months although autumn and winter seldom bite here. Christmas and New Year parties are very popular. Recently refurbished bedrooms are thoughtfully equipped with some on the ground floor suitable for the elderly or disabled. The cuisine is outstanding with a master chef creating an excellent choice of à la carte and table d'hôte menus of traditional English fare in which local specialities, particularly seafood and Cornish clotted cream, feature prominently. An old-fashioned English breakfast is served, whilst the Gwendra Room is the pleasant setting for light luncheons and Cornish cream teas which may also be enjoyed in the garden, on the terrace or by the swimming pool. Other sporting facilities include a new all-weather tennis court, a well-equipped games room, separate billiards room with full-size table, and an exercise room with sauna and solarium. Children are especially well catered for. There is a fine playroom and play area at their disposal and immediately fronting the hotel is a safe, sandy beach. *AA/RAC***, Egon Ronay, Johansen.*

PENMERE MANOR HOTEL

PENMERE MANOR HOTEL,
Mongleath Road, Falmouth, Cornwall TR11 4PN

Tel: 0326 211411
Fax: 0326 317588

Licensed; 39 bedrooms, all with private facilities; Historic interest; Children welcome, pets by arrangement; Car park (50); Truro 11 miles, Redruth 10; £££.

A fine Georgian house situated in five acres of gardens and woodland overlooking Falmouth Bay. Owned and managed by the Pope family for over 20 years, Penmere maintains the country house ambience throughout the public rooms and bedrooms. The superior Garden Rooms offer the last word in space, comfort and facilities. Excellent food in Bolitho's Restaurant is complemented by an extensive personally selected wine list, accompanied by entertainment from the grand piano. The Fountain Leisure Club offers leisure pursuits for all ages, with both indoor and outdoor swimming pools, mini-gym, sauna, solarium, croquet and even outdoor giant chess! Penmere guarantees a warm welcome and a peaceful and relaxing holiday or short break. *WCTB ✿ ✿ ✿ ✿ Commended, AA and RAC*** Country House.*

CORMORANT HOTEL,
Golant, Fowey,
Cornwall PL23 1LL

Tel and Fax: 0726 833426

Restaurant licence; 11 bedrooms, all with private bathrooms; Children over 12 years and dogs welcome; Car park (15); Fowey 2 miles; ££.

Perched 70 feet above the tidal reaches of the Fowey River, the Cormorant Hotel provides beautiful views from all its rooms of this source of excellent salmon and sea bass fishing. It offers a high standard of accommodation, all bedrooms having en suite bathroom and colour TV, while the restaurant is renowned for its superb cuisine. One delightful feature of the hotel is the heated swimming pool which has sliding glass doors and a motorised roof to allow for all moods of the weather. Golant is an unspoilt village with local facilities for sailing, fishing and golfing, as well as country walks and sandy beaches. *ETB* 👑 👑 👑 *Commended, AA**, RAC, Egon Ronay, Johansens.*

THE OLD MILL COUNTRY HOUSE,
Little Petherick, Near Padstow,
Cornwall PL27 7QT

Tel: 0841 540388*

Residential licence; 6 bedrooms; Historic interest; Pets welcome except in bedrooms; Car park (10); Wadebridge 4 miles; £.

This Grade II listed building is a 16th century converted corn mill complete with waterwheel that nestles next to a stream that feeds the Camel estuary. In a pretty garden, in a charming village, the Old Mill retains its character and charm whilst providing guests with modern amenities. The attractive little resort of Padstow with its picturesque harbour is just two miles away and there are many sandy beaches, coves and beautiful walks nearby. Personal attention is assured from Proprietors, Michael and Pat Walker and the dishes served in the Mill Room represent traditional cuisine at its best. The well-appointed bedrooms all have views of the countryside and most have en suite facilities. *RAC Acclaimed, AA QQQ.*

TRELAWNE HOTEL,
Mawnan Smith, Falmouth,
Cornwall TR11 5HS

Tel: 0326 250226*
Fax: 0326 250909

Licensed; 16 bedrooms, 14 with private bathrooms; Children and pets welcome; Car park (20); Truro 13 miles, Falmouth 5; ££.

Nestling on the coastline between the Helford and Fal rivers in a beautiful and tranquil corner of Cornwall, this fine country house hotel enjoys a magnificent outlook across Falmouth Bay to the Roseland Peninsula. Maenporth beach is but a short distance away and there are numerous idyllic coves nearby. The tastefully furnished and centrally heated bedrooms have en suite facilities, as well as colour television, radio, telephone and tea and coffee makers. There is a charming cocktail bar where new friends are easily made, and for recreation there is an indoor pool and games room. The cuisine comes high on the list of attractions at this well-run hotel, dishes being attractively prepared by award-winning chefs and backed by an extensive wine list. *ETB* 👑 👑 👑 👑, *AA***.*

BUDOCK VEAN GOLF AND COUNTRY HOUSE HOTEL,
Mawnan Smith, Near Falmouth, Cornwall TR11 5LG

Tel: 0326 250288*
Fax: 0326 250892

Residential and restaurant licence; 58 bedrooms, all with private bathrooms; Children welcome, pets allowed except in public rooms; Car park (70); Falmouth 4 miles; £££.

Set in 65 acres of sub-tropical grounds, Budock Vean offers comfortable and stylish accommodation, superb cuisine and an excellent selection of wines. Amenities include top-class all weather tennis courts, a spectacular indoor swimming pool, and a beautifully laid out private golf course. Visit this elegant hotel and enjoy a holiday with style. ✿ ✿ ✿ ✿ *Commended, AA and RAC***. **See also Colour Advertisement p.4.**

KERRYANNA COUNTRY HOUSE,
Treleaven Farm, Mevagissey, Cornwall PL26 6RZ

Tel: 0726 843558

Licensed; 6 bedrooms, all with private bathrooms; Children over 5 years welcome; Car park; Newquay 20 miles, St Austell 6; £.

Percy and Linda Hennah invite you to enjoy the peace and tranquillity at Kerryanna, surrounded by beautiful countryside, wild flowers and abundant wildlife. You can relax in the comfortable lounges and watch rabbits, pheasants and wild birds in their natural habitat. The thoughtfully furnished bedrooms are all en suite and have tea and coffee making facilities, colour television and central heating. Great pride is taken in the cuisine, with a choice of menu featuring fresh local produce, and delicious home-made desserts with clotted cream. Vegetarians are catered for, and there is a separate children's menu. Leisure facilities include an outdoor heated pool (May to September), a games barn and an 18-hole putting green; watersports and golf available nearby. *ETB* ✿ ✿ *Commended, AA Listed.*

TREGLOS HOTEL,
Constantine Bay, Padstow, Cornwall PL28 8JH

Tel: 0841 520727*
Fax: 0841 521163

Residential and restaurant licence; 44 bedrooms, all with private bathrooms; Children welcome, pets allowed except in public rooms; Car park (40), garages (8); Padstow 3 miles; ££.

Overlooking the sea and Trevose Golf Course, this superb hotel offers 44 bedrooms, all with bathrooms, colour television, direct-dial telephones and central heating. Amenities include an indoor heated pool and jacuzzi; leisure activities such as fishing, water sports and golf can be enjoyed nearby. Write or phone for colour brochure to owner/managers Mr and Mrs F.G. Barlow. *AA and RAC***, Egon Ronay, Ashley Courtenay and Signpost Recommended.* **See also Colour Advertisement p.4.**

HIGHER FAUGAN COUNTRY HOUSE HOTEL,
Newlyn, Penzance, Cornwall TR18 5HS

Tel: 0736 62076
Fax: 0736 51648

Residential and restaurant licence; 12 bedrooms, all with private bathrooms; Historic interest; Children and pets welcome; Car park (20); Helston 13 miles, St Ives 8; ££.

In 10 acres of parklike grounds with delightful views over Newlyn to Mounts Bay, this gracious and informal house is a holiday venue blessed with amenities which, in our own experience, are well above average and worthy of special recommendation. Guest rooms are individually and tastefully furnished, each having a private bath, direct-dial telephone, colour television, clock radio and tea and coffee-making facilities. Guests may laze in the grounds all day, enjoy a good bar lunch and a dip in the attractively-set outdoor pool or explore nearby beaches and beauty spots, returning to a memorable dinner featuring home-grown produce. One may end a pleasant day in the bar, watching television or playing snooker. *ETB* ✿ ✿ ✿ ✿, *AA ***.

CLAREMONT HOTEL,
Polperro,
Cornwall PL13 2RG

Tel: 0503 72241

Licensed; 11 bedrooms, all with private bathrooms; Children and pets welcome; Car park (16);
London 240 miles, Penzance 65, Plymouth 25, Looe 4; £.

Built around a seventeenth century cottage, the Claremont Hotel overlooks a valley in the heart of South Cornwall's most picturesque fishing village. It has its own private car park. It is ideally located for walking (along the cliffs), swimming in secluded coves, golfing and fishing, as well as exploring the rest of Cornwall. The rooms are fresh and intimate, with tea-making facilities, colour television and direct-dial telphone. The lounge bar and restaurant feel warm and comfortable and the service is friendly. From home-made shepherd's pies to an exclusive French menu, the kitchen caters for every taste and appetite. Ideal for a relaxing holiday, taking advantage of generous discounts for short and longer breaks. Pets are welcome. Open all year. *ETB* 👑 👑 👑, *AA and RAC*, Logis of Great Britain.*

ROSE-IN-VALE COUNTRY HOUSE HOTEL,
Mithian, St Agnes,
Cornwall TR5 0QD

Tel: 0872 552202
Fax: 0872 552700

Residential and restaurant licence; 17 bedrooms, all with private bathrooms; Car park (40);
Children and pets welcome; St Agnes 2 miles; ££.

Occupying a sheltered and secluded position in its own small valley amidst beautiful Cornish countryside and near the coast, this Georgian Country House Hotel has grounds extending to 11 acres including beautiful gardens, woodland and pasture as well as a heated swimming pool and sheltered sun terrace. Inside the house, guests will find bedrooms equipped with hairdryers, radio, television, tea-makers and telephones. Shower over bath in standard bedrooms and the Four Poster Suite. Excellent meals are served from table d'hôte and à la carte menus in the Trellis Restaurant overlooking the gardens. The hotel boasts a new games room and those wishing to venture a little further afield will find National Trust properties, beaches, golf courses, sporting facilities and night life within easy reach. *ETB* 👑 👑 👑 👑 *Commended, AA and RAC**, Ashley Courtenay Highly Recommended, Hospitality Hotels of Cornwall, Good Hotel Guide Recommended.* **See also Colour Advertisement p.4.**

The £ symbol when appearing at the end of the italic section of an entry shows the anticipated price, during 1993, for a **single room with English Breakfast.**

Under £30	£	**Over £45 but under £60** £££
Over £30 but under £45 ££		**Over £60** ££££

This is meant as an indication only and does not show prices for Special Breaks, Weekends, etc. Guests are therefore advised to verify all prices on enquiring or booking.

TREVAUNANCE POINT HOTEL,
Trevaunance Cove, St Agnes,
Cornwall TR5 0RZ

Tel: 087-255 3235

Residential and restaurant licence; 2 double bedrooms, 5 twin/family bedrooms, 1 single bedroom; Children and dogs welcome; Car park (20); Newquay 12 miles, Truro 8, Redruth 7; ££.

Take a step back in time and visit the centuries-old Trevaunance Point Hotel, nestling in clifftop gardens above the "lost harbour of St. Agnes", its windows gazing seaward across the wide expanse of Perran Bay. Built from granite, local stone and slate, and giant beams wrested by wreckers from ill-fated ships, the hotel in summer becomes a cool oasis, and in winter a warm and welcoming haven against the bracing and spectacular storms which often rage along this rugged Atlantic coastline. Not this hotel for those who seek the plastic standards of the twentieth century — but good food in abundance, professional but friendly and courteous service, crackling log fires and candlelit dinners, the constant vocal accompaniment of the ever-moving sea, a pace of life and many other things you thought had long since been lost. The hotel is open all year and can be highly recommended for spring and autumn holidays. Bargain weekend breaks are available, and a colour brochure may be obtained on request from Proprietor Marc Watts. *AA**.

DALSWINTON COUNTRY HOUSE HOTEL,
St Mawgan, Near Newquay,
Cornwall TR8 4EZ

Tel: 0637 860385

Residential and restaurant licence; 9 bedrooms, all with private bathrooms; Historic interest; Children and pets welcome; Car park (15); Padstow 6 miles, Newquay 5; £.

Approached by its own 200-yard drive, Dalswinton is an old Cornish house of immense character in one and a half acres of secluded grounds, overlooking the beautiful Valley of Lanherne with views to the sea. Ideally situated between Newquay and Padstow on what is reputed to be the finest coastline in Europe, with superb beaches and coastal walks within two miles. The hotel has been completely refurbished and offers superb food in a friendly, comfortable atmosphere. All rooms are en suite and centrally heated, with television and tea/coffee making facilities. Log fires in bar and lounge. There is a heated swimming pool. Open all year, including Christmas and New Year. Colour brochure available on request. *ETB* ♥♥♥, *AA***.

BOSSINEY HOUSE HOTEL,
Tintagel,
Cornwall PL34 0AX

Tel: 0840 770240*

Residential and restaurant licence; 20 bedrooms, all en-suite; Children and dogs welcome; Car park (30); Bodmin 20 miles, Bude 19, Camelford 6; £.

At one time Bossiney had its own mayor and corporation, and in the 16th century Sir Francis Drake was one of its two MPs. Today a cluster of houses nestle close to a sandy cove with interesting rock formations, ideal for bathing, surfing or just unwinding. With wonderful cliff walks on either side this is the glorious situation of the beautifully furnished Bossiney House Hotel, standing in grounds of two and a half acres. Guests may relax in the gardens, the indoor heated swimming pool, the sauna or solarium; take in the sweeping sea views; or try their skills on the putting green. Inside, one is immediately impressed by the spacious cleanliness of the public and private rooms, and in particular by the imaginative and pleasing colour schemes. This is a really happy place in which to stay, and the proprietors and staff work hard to achieve this end. Pleasant lounges, one with a bar, are convivial meeting places in which to enjoy refreshment; the well-appointed bedrooms make the most of sea and country views. In the catering department, fine English cooking is a feature of the menus which offer excellent choice and variety. Quaint Tintagel is near at hand, and the surrounding King Arthur's country provides an almost bewildering choice of beauty spots, historic locations and sporting activities.

Cumbria

LOWBYER MANOR COUNTRY HOUSE HOTEL,
Hexham Road, Alston,
Cumbria CA9 3JX

Tel: 0434 381230
Fax: 0434 382937

Restaurant and residential licence; 11 bedrooms, all with private bathrooms; Historic interest;
Children over 8 years welcome, pets by arrangement; Car park (14); Penrith 19 miles; £.

Nestling below the unspoilt fells and peaks of the High Pennines, this stone-built former mansion house provides comfort, good company and all the requisites for a peaceful and revivifying holiday under the aegis of Peter and Margaret Hughes. Guest rooms have either bath or toilet and shower en suite, colour television, radio and hospitality tray. In a country house party setting, new friends are easily made in a delightful bar with natural stone walls and oak beams whilst there is an exciting selection of à la carte English and Continental dishes on offer in the adjacent Derwent Restaurant. Alston is a charming little town and there is much in the area to attract hill or riverside walkers, bird watchers and botanists. 🌷🌷🌷, *AA and RAC**, Signpost, Ashley Courtenay.*

KIRKSTONE FOOT COUNTRY HOUSE HOTEL,
Kirkstone Pass Road, Ambleside,
Cumbria LA22 9EH
Tel: 05394 32232

Residential and restaurant licence; 16 bedrooms, all with private bathrooms; 16 self-catering apartments; Children welcome; Car park (25); Penrith 30 miles, Keswick 17, Kendal 13; DB&B ££.

Originally a seventeenth century manor house, this attractively furnished hotel stands in delightful, secluded grounds at the foot of one of Lakeland's most famous passes, yet is conveniently only a few minutes' walk from Ambleside village, the ideal centre from which to explore the English Lake District. In the hotel Annabel and Andrew Bedford continue traditions in providing superb food and gracious living in a convivial atmosphere, where traditional English home cooking and a fine cellar are widely acclaimed. Dining at the Kirkstone Foot is an experience you will long remember. Additionally, for those who prefer a greater degree of independence on holiday, there are several luxurious self-contained apartments within the grounds of the hotel, each of which is fully equipped, including colour television and full central heating. Guests are welcome to enjoy all the amenities of the hotel, and pets are welcome in the apartments. Open Christmas and New Year. *ETB* 👑 👑 👑 👑, *BTA Commended.*

APPLEBY MANOR COUNTRY HOUSE HOTEL,
Roman Road, Appleby-in-Westmorland,
Cumbria CA16 6JD
Tel: 076-83 51571

Fully licensed; 30 bedrooms, all with private bathrooms; Historic interest; Children and pets welcome; Car park (50); Kendal 24 miles, Penrith 13, Brough 8; ££/£££.

Set in wooded grounds overlooking Appleby's fine castle, with panoramic views of the Pennines and Eden Valley, Appleby Manor is a hotel in which you will feel immediately at home. Where nicer to return to after a great day out in the Lakes or Yorkshire Dales than this relaxing and friendly country house with its log fires, beautiful public rooms and high quality, fully equipped bedrooms. Take a refreshing dip in the heated indoor pool in the leisure club before enjoying a superb meal in the renowned restaurant, and then retiring to one of the comfy chairs in the lounge with a malt whisky selected from a choice of over 70. 👑 👑 👑 👑 *Highly Commended, AA and RAC ***.*

LINDETH HOWE HOTEL,
Storrs Park, Bowness-on-Windermere,
Cumbria LA23 3JF

Tel: 05394 45759
Fax: 05394 46368

Licensed; 14 bedrooms, all with private bathrooms; Historic interest; Kendal 9 miles, Windermere 1; ££.

"A little gem hidden away" as quoted by Ashley Courtenay. The hotel occupies an impressive position overlooking Lake Windermere, and stands in six acres of its own lovely grounds. Built in 1879, it was once the home of Beatrix Potter, who bought it for her mother, and where she spent many holidays enjoying its unrivalled views and idyllic location. Many of the rooms take advantage of the splendid views across the lake, and all have colour television, radio, telephone, tea/coffee making facilities and central heating. The elegant dining room is the perfect place to enjoy a candlelit dinner with a tempting choice of exciting dishes, relaxing afterwards in the lounge over coffee by the log fire in the inglenook fireplace. For the more energetic, the hotel has an exercise area, sauna and solarium. Short breaks available. *ETB* 🦢🦢🦢🦢 *Commended, RAC Commended, Les Routiers recommended.*

HAYTON HALL HOTEL,
Near Wetheral, Carlisle,
Cumbria CA4 8QD

Tel: 0228 70651
Fax: 0228 70010

Fully licensed; 17 bedrooms, all with private bathrooms; Historic interest; Children welcome, pets by arrangement; Car park (200); Carlisle 4 miles; ££££.

Recently superbly refurbished throughout, this fine country house hotel on the A69 offers facilities which are sheer delight. Guest rooms are luxuriously appointed; lavish drapes adorn the bedheads and windows and all the amenities are there that one would expect in a luxury 4-star hotel. Some rooms have private spa baths and the Bridal Boudoirs have four-poster beds. An award-winning master chef holds sway in the matter of cuisine, producing dishes and suitable wines of the highest calibre. The hotel stands resplendent in 68 acres of park and woodland featuring ornamental lakes and formal rose gardens — a romantic setting indeed. In the courtyard is the 'Famous Lord Edmond' where one may obtain entrées, bar meals and local beers. 🦢🦢🦢🦢🦢 *Highly Commended, RAC and AA ****.*

AYNSOME MANOR HOTEL,
Cartmel, Near Grange-over-Sands,
Cumbria LA11 6HH

Tel: 053-95 36653*
Fax: 053-95 36016

Restaurant and residential licence; 13 bedrooms, 12 with private bathrooms; Historic interest; Well-behaved children and pets welcome; Car park (20); Grange-over-Sands 2 miles; DB&B £££.

Beckoning the discriminating country lover, particularly those who appreciate superb home cooking, Aynsome Manor has a happy and informal air and enjoys a lovely setting just four miles from Lake Windermere. Rooms are delightfully furnished and bedroom amenities include colour television, radio/alarm, direct-dial telephone and tea and coffee-makers. Central heating and cheerful log fires ensure added comfort for those taking spring and autumn holidays. The Varley family personally supervise the well-being of guests and, assisted by a friendly and able staff, present an impeccable cuisine. Dining is by candlelight in elegant surroundings and the sumptuous sweet trolley will tempt the most obdurate palate. Cartmel is a charming village noted for its 12th century priory. 🦢🦢🦢🦢, *AA **.*

ULLSWATER HOTEL,
Glenridding, Penrith,
Cumbria CA11 0PA

Tel: 07684 82444

Fax: 07684 82303

Fully licensed; 48 bedrooms, all with private bathrooms; Children and pets welcome; Car park (100); Patterdale one mile; ££.

With its wide and most imposing facade, this fine hotel dates from mid-Victorian times although every modern convenience has been incorporated with subtle taste to charm those who seek tranquillity in beautiful surroundings and the ultimate in comfort and friendly service. Set in 20 acres of lovely grounds, the hotel makes the most of its wonderful lakeside situation. From its windows the views are breathtaking, especially from the main restaurant (seating 120) where full table d'hôte and à la carte menus are on offer. Lounge bar meals and hikers' meals are also served and children, who have their own playground area, may have an evening meal served in bedroom or lounge. Tastefully designed in a variety of styles, guest rooms of all sizes are available from honeymoon and four-poster rooms to singles. All, however, have the same excellent amenities — private facilities, central heating, radio, telephone and tea and coffee-makers and colour television is also available. Two ground-floor rooms are especially suitable for disabled guests. There are two spacious and comfortable lounges, two bars, television lounge, launderette and a lift. In the superb grounds is a 9-hole pitch and putt course and boat launching facilities; in all, everything to provide a carefree vacation 'par excellence'. 🏆 🏆 🏆 🏆 *Commended.*

WILD BOAR HOTEL,
Crook, Near Windermere,
Cumbria LA23 3NF

Tel: 05394 45225
Fax: 05394 42498

Fully licensed; 36 bedrooms, including 2 luxury suites, all with private bathrooms; Historic interest; Children welcome; Car park; Ambleside 7 miles, Kendal 6; £££.

Set in the lovely Gilpin Valley, just three miles from the shores of Lake Windermere, this former 19th century coaching inn is ideally placed for exploring the wonderful scenery and many places of interest in the Lake District. The beautifully decorated bedrooms have every modern facility, including remote-control television and telephone, and the cosy public rooms have low oak beams and open log fires. The attractive candlelit dining room offers an excellent selection of delicious dishes. Guests have full use of the leisure facilities at the Low Wood Hotel, including swimming pool, fitness centre, squash courts and health club. ✿ ✿ ✿ ✿ *Commended, AA/RAC***.*

HAMPSFELL HOUSE HOTEL,
Hampsfell Road, Grange-over-Sands,
Cumbria LA11 6BG

Tel: 05395 32567*

Fully licensed; 9 bedrooms, 7 with private bathrooms; Children and pets welcome; Car park (20); Lancaster 24 miles, Ambleside 19; £.

Just half-a-mile from the centre of the small and charming resort of Grange, this happy and comfortable little hotel stands in 2 acres of grounds on the fringe of Eggerslack Woods. As an ideal centre for exploring the Lake District and the multifarious attractions of the Cartmel and Furness Peninsulas, this is a venue that is well recommended for the excellence of its home-cooked food, accommodation and general ambience. Central heating is installed throughout and there is a cosy bar where a fire adds its cheer on cooler days. Most of the well-furnished bedrooms have private facilities as well as colour television and tea and coffee-makers. Terms are very reasonable. ✿ ✿ ✿ *Commended, AA**, Ashley Courtenay.*

RED HOUSE HOTEL,
Underskiddaw, Near Keswick,
Cumbria CA12 4QA
Tel: 07687 72211

Residential and restaurant licence; 22 bedrooms, all with private bathrooms; Children and dogs welcome; Parking (25); Carlisle 25 miles, Penrith 16; £.

Beautifully situated two miles north of Keswick with commanding panoramic views over Lakeland, the extensive wooded grounds offer seclusion in which to relax. The friendly atmosphere, deliciously tempting food and comfortable surroundings in this Victorian country house provide the right background for an enjoyable holiday. Socially acceptable dogs are welcomed. Please ask for our brochure to see how you would benefit from the lifestyle at Red House. *AA and RAC**, Ashley Courtenay Recommended.*

DALE HEAD HALL LAKESIDE HOTEL,
Lake Thirlmere, Keswick,
Cumbria CA12 4TN
Tel: 07687 72478

Restaurant and residential licence; 9 bedrooms, all with private bathrooms; Historic interest; Children welcome; Car park (20); Keswick 4 miles, Grasmere 4; ££.

Those seeking respite from the hustle and bustle of day-to-day living will find true peace and tranquillity at this exceptional hotel, where resident proprietors, Alan and Shirley Lowe, place the emphasis most firmly on comfort and relaxation. Standing alone on the shores of the lake and enjoying magnificent views from bedroom, bar and lounge, Dale Head Hall provides accommodation of the highest standard. All rooms have private bathroom and are individually furnished. After a relaxing day, perhaps spent exploring the acres of delightful garden, woodland or shoreline, what finer prospect than a delicious five-course dinner prepared using wholesome produce brought fresh from the walled kitchen garden. *Cumbria Tourist Board* 🌸 🌸 🌸 🌸 *Highly Commended, AA and RAC**, Johansens.*

LADSTOCK COUNTRY HOUSE HOTEL,
Thornthwaite, Keswick,
Cumbria CA12 5RZ
Tel: 07687 78210

Fully licensed; 20 bedrooms, 16 with private bathrooms; Historic interest; Children welcome; Car park (100); Keswick 3 miles; ££.

Nestling on a hillside, snug in its 12 acres of lovely woooded grounds, this one-time vicarage gazes down on Bassenthwaite Lake, with the magnificence of Skiddaw rising beyond. Built over 200 years ago but later extended, this is a listed building that offers a high standard of amenities for the benefit of its guests. Lounges and bedrooms are richly furnished in both antique and modern style, the latter being individually decorated and most having bath or shower en suite, colour television and tea and coffee making facilities. Spacious four-poster or half-tester rooms are ideal for honeymoons and special occasions. Excellent traditional English fare is served and prices at this recommended Lakeland venue are very reasonable. 🌸 🌸 🌸 *Commended, AA and RAC**, Ashley Courtenay.*

DERWENTWATER HOTEL,
Portinscale, Keswick,
Cumbria CA12 5RE

Tel: 07687 72538

Fax: 07687 71002

Fully licensed; 84 bedrooms, all with private bathrooms; Children and pets welcome; Car park (120); Keswick 1 mile; £££.

Situated in 16 acres of delightful mature grounds on the shores of Lake Derwentwater, the hotel accommodates guests in 84 en suite bedrooms, many with lake view. Colour television, radio, trouser press, hair dryer, telephone and tea/coffee making facilities are included. Single rooms and a four-poster suite complete the choice available. An excellent menu is offered in the Deer's Leap Restaurant and guests can relax in either of the two lounges or our superb conservatory. Although the hotel is centrally heated throughout, log fires bring cheer to colder days. For leisure hours there is a putting green and private fishing available. A children's play area and baby listening complement family visitors. Telephone our helpful receptionist for colour brochure and tariff. 🌷 🌷 🌷 🌷, *AA and RAC***.*

THWAITE HOWE HOTEL,
Thornthwaite, Near Keswick,
Cumbria CA12 5SA

Tel: 07687 78281*

Restaurant and residential licence; 8 bedrooms, all with private bathrooms; Children over 12 and well-behaved dogs welcome; Car park (12); Keswick 3 miles; £.

This lovely stone-built and centrally heated country hotel enjoys magnificent views across to Skiddaw and the surrounding mountains and provides the ideal venue for a peaceful and relaxing holiday. All bedrooms have colour television, radio, tea and coffee making facilities and direct-dial telephones. The comfortable residents' lounge and the dining room take full advantage of the views, and both the lounge and the intimate bar have open fires. This is an excellent base from which to explore the whole of the Lake District whilst benefiting from a location amongst the quieter Northern Fells. The resident proprietors Mike and Penny Sutton offer you a warm welcome and an informal and friendly atmosphere, with good home cooking and quality wines at value-for-money prices. *ETB* 🌷 🌷 🌷 *Commended, AA and RAC**, Ashley Courtenay Recommended.*

WASDALE HEAD INN,
Wasdale Head, Near Gosforth, Cumbria CA20 1EX

Tel: 09467 26229
Fax: 09467 26334*

Licensed; 10 bedrooms, all with private bathrooms; Children and dogs welcome; Car park (50); Whitehaven 21 miles; DB&B £££.

Standing in a unique and secluded setting at the head of Wasdale is this fine Inn, which embodies something of the spirit of adventure that attracted smugglers, mountaineers, and finally tourists to this valley, one of Lakeland's most remote and unspoilt. All the individually decorated bedrooms enjoy magnificent mountain views, while public rooms exude a warmth rarely found in the more stereotyped chain hotels of today. The culinary emphasis is on good home cooking, with a hearty breakfast in the morning and five-course table d'hôte in the evening. There is a wealth of leisure pursuits in this lovely area. *ETB* 🌷 🌷 🌷 🌷, *AA and RAC **.*

GREENHILL LODGE HOTEL,
Red Dial, Wigton, Cumbria CA7 8LS

Tel: 06973 43304

Fully licensed; 7 bedrooms, all with private bathrooms; Historic interest; Pets welcome; Car park (100); Carlisle 11 miles; ££.

With the options of visiting the Lake District or the verdant Lowlands of Scotland, this is a charming 18th century mansion with an enthusiastic staff and, as we discovered, a reputation for good company and food. Elegantly furnished, the house stands in 10 acres of parkland incorporating a 9-hole pitch and putt course which has an obvious appeal to guests of all ages. An attractive lounge bar and an unusual cellar bar, created from a centuries-old keep, have their adherents. A sweeping Georgian staircase leads to spacious, delightfully appointed bedrooms, all with en suite amenities, colour television, direct-dial telephone and tea and coffee-making facilities. The hotel also caters well for conferences, social functions and weddings. *AA **, Ashley Courtenay.*

QUARRY GARTH COUNTRY HOUSE HOTEL,
Troutbeck Bridge, Windermere, Cumbria LA23 1LF

Tel: 05394 88282

Residential and restaurant licence; 10 bedrooms, all with private bathrooms; Children and pets welcome; Car park (30); Penrith 26 miles, Kendal 8, Ambleside 3; ££.

An elegant hotel with charm and style, Quarry Garth is set in eight peaceful acres of garden and grounds amid shrubs and wild flowers, adding to the air of tranquillity and relaxation for which guests return again and again. Resident proprietors, Huw and Lynne Phillips, run the hotel in true country house style, offering personal service and calm, warm comfort in a background of log fires and rich oak panelling. Individually designed bedrooms all have en suite facilities, central heating, radio and colour television, tea and coffee makers and direct-dial telephone. The restaurant's superb cuisine offers the best of local fresh produce prepared with imaginative flair. 🌷 🌷 🌷 *Highly Commended, AA **.*

MILLER HOWE HOTEL,
**Rayrigg Road, Windermere,
Cumbria LA23 1EY**

Tel: 05394 42536*
Fax: 05394 45664

Residential licence; 13 bedrooms, all with private bathrooms; Pets welcome; Car park; Kendal 8 miles, Ambleside 5; ££££.

Known for the distinctive 'Tovey Touch', Miller Howe is a culinary dream come true. As one national daily newspaper quoted: 'At Miller Howe you are welcomed, lapped in luxury and fed — almost overfed — with dedication'; a perfect description. Proprietor John Tovey has won accolades galore for his epicurean skills and Residential Cookery Courses along with Spring and Autumn Breaks are now regular features. But a little about the hotel itself. This is an elegant Edwardian country house immediately overlooking Lake Windermere, the perfect place in which to relax and enjoy the good things of life. Bedrooms all have private facilities, ideal for restful repose after a day's activities and dining regally — in the best possible taste.

Derbyshire

CAVENDISH HOTEL,
**Baslow,
Derbyshire DE4 1SP**

Tel: 0246 582311
Fax: 0246 582312

Fully licensed; 23 bedrooms, all with private bathrooms; Historic interest; Children welcome; Car park (50); Sheffield 12 miles, Matlock 9.

With a history as an inn which goes back over 200 years, the comely Cavendish is luxuriously and warmly appointed throughout and it is obvious that Proprietor, Eric Marsh, has put his 30-plus years experience as a hotelier to the most effective use; furthermore, he is well supported by a willing and efficient staff. Guest rooms are beautifully equipped with twin or double beds, colour television, direct-dial telephone, clock radio, refrigerated bar, bathroom with shower as well as numerous thoughtful extras. The attraction of the public rooms is enhanced by a collection of over 300 pictures. Breakfast may be taken any time in the morning and lunch formally or casually in the restaurant or garden room, whilst dinner is a delight that almost defies description. ♛ ♛ ♛ ♛, *AA 3 Red Stars, RAC*** and Blue Riband.*

THE WIND IN THE WILLOWS,
Derbyshire Level, Glossop,
Derbyshire SK13 9PT

Tel: 0457 868001
Fax: 0457 853354

Residential licence; 8 bedrooms, all with private bathrooms; Historic interest; Children welcome; Car park (20); Manchester 13 miles; £££.

A haven of tranquillity in the Peak District National Park, this homely Victorian country house stands in 5 acres of grounds and from its windows are spectacular views of the Snake Pass and grouse moors. Yet, for all its apparent remoteness, the little town of Glossop is only a mile away. Charmingly appointed, far removed from urban clamour, relaxation is easily acquired amidst oak panelling, open fires and traditional furnishings. Anne and Peter Marsh pay unobtrusive attention to the comfort of their guests and excellent home cooking is another cause to celebrate. All rooms have twin or double beds and feature en suite shower and/or bath, colour television, direct-dial telephone, hot drinks facility and a host of other thoughtful extras. ♛♛♛ *Highly Commended, AA **, RAC "Best Small Hotel in the North", Johansen.*

RIBER HALL,
Matlock,
Derbyshire DE4 5JU

Tel: 0629 582795
Fax: 0629 580475

Restaurant and residential licence; 11 bedrooms, all with private bathrooms; Historic interest; Children over 10 years welcome; Car park; Sheffield 24 miles, Derby 18, Ashbourne 14; ££££.

A rare opportunity to recapture the grace and charm of the Elizabethan era exists in the heart of peaceful Derbyshire countryside. This lovely old manor house, a Listed building dating from the 15th century, with a superb, peaceful, old walled garden, presents luxurious accommodation in half-timbered bedrooms with antique four-poster beds. Comfort is assured by such modern amenities as central heating, colour television and direct-dial telephone. All rooms have en suite facilities. The restaurant is renowned for its fine cuisine and excellent wine list, the pleasures of which are enhanced by attentive service and intriguing period decor. Tennis can be enjoyed in the grounds, and clay pigeon shooting nearby, and there are many historic houses in the area well worth a visit. Featured in all leading guides. ****, Egon Ronay Coffee Award.*

BREADSALL PRIORY HOTEL, GOLF AND COUNTRY CLUB,
Moor Road, Morley,
Derbyshire DE7 6DL

Tel: 0332 832235
Fax: 0332 833509

Fully licensed; 91 bedrooms, all with private bathrooms; Historic interest; Children welcome; Car park (300); Derby 4 miles; ££££.

Rich history and ancient traditions echo throughout this imposing old Priory which dates back to the 15th century. Today, time-scarred battlements look out over 200 acres of parkland with an ornamental lake and two excellent 18-hole golf courses. Ancient the mellow building may be, but the finest contemporary amenities have been introduced to serve modern-day guests. In addition, there are such impressive leisure facilities as an indoor heated swimming pool, squash and tennis courts and a fitness studio with opportunities to relax in jacuzzi, sauna, solarium or health and beauty salon. Active pursuits promote sharpened appetites and these are well catered for by the enlightened cuisine. ♛♛♛♛ *, AA***.*

**If you've found
RECOMMENDED COUNTRY HOTELS
of service please tell your friends**

Sunday 19th. night σ

Tariff. double room ensite. £95 - £120

Brochure   B&B

12 Fallow Close   MH
Dodworth
Barnsley
S75 3TE

01226 293410.

Address.

⇒ 19th May — rooms £75 room.

Internet

Compuserve
1st 5 hours free via membership
after that £2 ph·

hat £12 pn·

advantage
15 mins

Carlos Hall Country HO
01335 343403

Hassop Hall

20th May 10·30
Robert

PARK HALL HOTEL,
Spinkhill,
Derbyshire S31 9YD

Tel: 0246 434897
Fax: 0246 436282

Fully licensed; 9 bedrooms, all with private bathrooms; Historic interest; Children welcome; Car park; Chesterfield 9 miles, Sheffield 9; £££.

A secluded 16th century manor house hotel set in eight and a half acres of delightful grounds, Park Hall is convenient for Chatsworth House, the Peak District and "Robin Hood" country. All guest rooms have colour television, trouser press, direct-dial telephone, hairdryer and tea and coffee making facilities. Only the freshest local produce is used in the elegant Uplands Manor Restaurant where an extensive wine list includes some fine old wines from France. Roaring log fires in winter, and croquet and bowling in the summer make it a haven in which to relax and soak up the delightful atmosphere of this former ancestral home. Resident owners, Tony and Jan Clark, and their staff look forward to offering a full measure of Spinkhillian hospitality. *EMTB* 🌷 🌷 🌷 🌷, *AA and RAC***.*

Devon

BOVEY HOUSE HOTEL,
Beer, Seaton,
Devon EX12 3AD

Tel: 029-780 241

Restaurant and residential licence; 12 bedrooms, 8 with private bathrooms; Historic interest; Children and dogs welcome; Car park (50); Exeter 22 miles, Sidmouth 9; £.

Of considerable historic interest, this sixteenth-century manor house has been beautifully converted to serve the needs of modern day guests, yet retains many ancient features. In three acres of peaceful grounds, the house is approached down a tree-lined drive, and immediately one enters the panelled Jacobean reception area one is captivated by the aura of a hallowed past. The oldest part is the present drawing room, once the medieval hall, and the adjacent Inglenooks Bar has a huge fifteenth-century fireplace. The superb dining room sets the scene for the delicious à la carte and table d'hôte cuisine. *Ashley Courtenay Recommended.*

GREAT TREE HOTEL,
Sandy Park, Near Chagford,
Devon TQ13 8JS

Tel: 0647 432491

Licensed; 12 bedrooms, all with private bathrooms; Well-behaved children and dogs welcome; Car park (40); Drewsteignton 2 miles; ££/£££.

An idyllic situation, quiet and very secluded, situated as it is in 18 acres of its own gardens and woods in the Dartmoor foothills. There are splendid views from the spacious lounge with its beams, beautifully carved oak stairway, and log fires (no problem with logs here!). There is a cosy bar and a small, intimate dining room, which is serviced by chefs with a leaning towards traditional menus and who obtain much of their ingredients straight from the hotel's own gardens or from local farmers. Most of the rooms are on the ground floor, face south, and enjoy magnificent views over the gardens and surrounding countryside. All are comfortably furnished, with private bathrooms, colour television, tea and coffee making facilities and private telephones. A homely and friendly atmosphere, a delightful place to unwind. *ETB* ❀ ❀ ❀ ❀, *RAC****. **See also Colour Advertisement p.6.**

HIGHBULLEN HOTEL,
Chittlehamholt, Umberleigh,
Devon EX37 9HD

Tel: 0769 540561
Fax: 0769 540492

Licensed; 35 bedrooms, all with private bathrooms; Children over 8 years welcome; South Molton 6 miles; ££££.

Highbullen, a splendid Victorian Gothic mansion stands on high ground in sixty acres of parkland, with fine views over the surrounding countryside. Life here is informal with many quiet hideaways. The extensive cellars are now the social and gastronomic heart of the hotel. The restaurant serving an excellent table d'hôte dinner with wide choice has appeared in all the reputable guides for over 25 years. All bedrooms have private bathroom, colour television, and direct dial telephone. Many are situated in the Home Farm and converted cottages within the grounds. INDOOR and outdoor tennis, UNLIMITED FREE GOLF on the 9-hole par 31 course (professional's shop). Squash, croquet and billiards. Massage and hairdressing by arrangement. Indoor and outdoor swimming pools, sauna, steam-room, spa-bath, sunbed and indoor putting green. **See also Colour Advertisement p.7.**

KITTIWELL HOUSE HOTEL,
Croyde,
Devon EX33 1PG

Tel: 0271 890247*
Fax: 0271 890469

Hotel and restaurant licence; 12 bedrooms, all with private bathrooms; Historic interest; Children and pets welcome; Car park (20); Barnstaple 10 miles, Ilfracombe 9; ££.

The charming old world facade of Kittiwell gives a fairy-story hint of the warmth, comfort and hospitality to be found within. Privately run by Resident Proprietors, Yvonne and Jim Lang, this 16th century thatched Devon longhouse has been sympathetically restored in such a manner that the fine modern facilities enhance rather than detract from its lovely old-world character. Slumbering in a deep valley, the hotel is within minutes of three golden beaches and National Trust cliff walks. Bedrooms, all centrally heated, have been recently refurbished; they all have private amenities and some are available with four-poster beds. A heavily beamed restaurant seats 40 people and the table d'hôte and extensive à la carte menus are skilfully prepared and delightfully presented by our Chef de Cuisine. ❀ ❀ ❀ ❀ *Highly Commended, AA/RAC** and Merit Awards, Johansen, Ashley Courtenay.*

FAIRWATER HEAD COUNTRY HOUSE HOTEL,
Hawkchurch,
Devon EX13 5TX
Tel: 0297 678349*

Licensed; 20 bedrooms, all with private bathrooms; Children and dogs welcome; Car park (30); Lyme Regis 5 miles, Axminster 3; ££££.

A peaceful country house with magnificent views across the Axe valley and set in one of Ashley Courtenay's "best ten hotel gardens in Britain". No conferences or wedding receptions or taped background music. Award-winning restaurant and highest rated AA*** hotel in the area. Family hospitality. Golf at reduced green fees at Lyme Regis, and endless places of interest nearby. *ETB* 🏵 🏵 🏵 🏵. **See also Colour Advertisement p.6.**

THE BEL ALP HOUSE,
Haytor, Near Bovey Tracey,
Devon TQ13 9XX
Tel: 0364 661217*

Residential and restaurant licence; 9 bedrooms, all with private bathrooms; Children and pets welcome; Car park (20); Plymouth 33 miles, Exeter 14; ££££.

This happily-placed and elegant Edwardian country mansion is, in essence, a magnificently furnished family house that has opened its doors for the delectation of guests. Lovingly cared for by the Curnock family, the house holds many architectural delights characterised by sweeping arches, an impressive oak staircase and high-ceilinged and spacious rooms to which the warm decor, rich furnishings and antiques act as the perfect complement. Nestling in beautiful grounds on the hillside, 900 feet up on the fringe of Dartmoor, the house enjoys breathtaking views. Here the highest standards of comfort, hospitality and good food obtain — all the ingredients for a perfect holiday in a perfect setting. With all three "Merit Awards" at Three Stars from both the AA and RAC, and "Highly Commended" grading and Four Crowns from the Tourist Board.

BUCKLAND-TOUT-SAINTS HOTEL,
Goveton, Kingsbridge,
Devon TQ7 2DS
Tel: 0548 853055*
Fax: 0548 856261

Restaurant and residential licence; 12 bedrooms, all with private bathrooms; Historic interest; Children over 8 years welcome, pets in grounds only; Car park (12); Kingsbridge 2 miles; £££.

A gracious Queen Anne manor house of immense charm, Buckland-Tout-Saints has adapted magnificently to its role as a country hotel of character and now provides the highest standards of comfort, cuisine and amenities for its discerning guests. In tranquil surroundings and standing resplendent in seven acres of beautiful gardens, this superb hotel is within easy reach of the coast, Dartmoor and many places of sporting and historic interest. Each suite and bedroom is in the de luxe class with a private bathroom, colour television, direct-dial telephone and a host of practical extras as standard. The cuisine is impressive and imaginative, meals being served in a 17th century panelled Queen Anne Restaurant with an extensive range of wines in support. *AA ***.*

LYDFORD HOUSE HOTEL,
Lydford, Okehampton,
Devon EX20 4AU

Tel: 082-282 347
Fax: 082-282 442

Licensed; 13 bedrooms, all with private bathrooms; Children over 5 welcome; Car park (30); Exeter 33 miles, Plymouth 25; £.

On the fringe of Dartmoor, this splendid early Victorian house is one of the finest country hotels in the area. Centrally heated throughout, the delightful guest rooms all have colour television, direct-dial telephones, radio, tea/coffee making facilities, and private bathrooms and WCs. Food here is a high priority, starting with a full English breakfast and concluding with a superb dinner, with a wide choice at each course. There is a comfortable lounge, with a log fire in winter, and a cosy cocktail bar with lounge adjoining. Fishing and golfing enthusiasts are well catered for nearby. The hotel has its own stables in the grounds, serving riders of all ages and abilities. Inclusive riding holidays or riding by the hour is offered for the entire family at reasonable rates. *ETB* 👑 👑 👑 👑.

LYNTON COTTAGE HOTEL,
North Walk Hill, Lynton,
Devon EX35 6ED

Tel: 0598 52342*
Fax: 0598 52597

Fully licensed; 17 bedrooms, all with private bathrooms; Pets welcome; Car park (20); Barnstaple 14 miles; £££.

Blessed with striking views of Exmoor, the Lyn Valley and Lynmouth Bay, the elegant Lynton Cottage Hotel claims prominence not only for its delectable and dominant position, but also for its comforts, service and cuisine. Delightfully appointed throughout, the hotel exudes a warm and friendly atmosphere and the furnishings are a joy to behold. Luxury and convenience epitomise the qualities of the individually decorated guest rooms, all of which have private facilities. The restaurant presents a wide variety of dishes which display imagination and excellence. A fine selection of moderately priced wines awaits to enhance the chef's art. This is a romantic retreat, the real antidote to urban strife. Special Gastronomic and Whodunit Weekends are organised out of the main season. *AA and RAC ****.

NICHOLS NYMET HOUSE,
North Tawton,
Devon EX20 2BP

Tel: 0837 82626*

Licensed; 8 bedrooms, all with private bathrooms; Historic interest; Children welcome; Car park (30); Okehampton 6 miles; £.

An especially fine example of a Georgian manor house, this lovely pink-washed Grade II listed building lies well back from the Crediton–Okehampton road between Exmoor and Dartmoor in its own woodland grounds which offer peace and relaxation. A haven of rest, comfort and good food, the house is the perfect base for exploring the countless beauties of the West Country. Guest rooms are well-appointed and all have bath or shower en suite. Nearby are good opportunities for golf, riding and fishing and the surrounding countryside is excellent walking terrain. Terms for a rewarding stay at this idyllic retreat represent excellent value.

HERON HOUSE HOTEL,
Thurlestone Sands, Salcombe,
Devon TQ7 3JY

Tel: 0548 561308
Fax: 0548 560180

Licensed; 18 bedrooms, all with private bathrooms; Children and pets welcome; Car park; Totnes 11 miles; £££.

In an unrivalled position at the edge of the sea and surrounded by unspoilt countryside, Heron House Hotel enjoys superb coastal and rural views. The beautifully appointed bedrooms are all en suite and have colour television, direct-dial telephone, radio and tea/coffee making facilities. Personally supervised by the Proprietor, first-class cuisine is served in the dining room, with Devon produce a speciality. For relaxation there is a comfortable bar lounge and a separate quiet lounge. The large outdoor swimming pool is heated from May to September. Guests are assured of a warm welcome and personal service from the Rowland family. Off-season breaks available. *ETB* 🌸 🌸 🌸 🌸, *Ashley Courtenay Recommended.*

BOLT HEAD HOTEL,
Sharpitor, Salcombe,
Devon TQ8 8LL

Tel: 0548 843751

Fax: 0548 843060

Fully licensed; 28 bedrooms, all with private bathrooms; Children welcome, pets by arrangement; Car park (30); Plymouth 22 miles; £££.

The nearest approach to a Mediterranean holiday in England, this delightful timber-built hotel enjoys a magnificent outlook over the Salcombe estuary and sea. Here, adjoining National Trust clifftop property, where the climate is so mild that oranges and lemons have been known to grow out of doors, the Bolt Head Hotel has a countrywide reputation for its accommodation, food, leisure activities and service. Bright and beautifully decorated, the hotel specialises in English and French cuisine with freshly caught fish, lobster and crab delivered daily from local trawlers and fresh farm produce and locally-made cheeses. To support these gastronomic delights is an extensive selection of wines. A light and sunny lounge and adjoining sun terrace with far-reaching views are ideal places in which to relax and enjoy a drink. The spruce pine-furnished guest rooms all have Laura Ashley decor, bathrooms en suite, colour television with satellite, radio and direct-dial telephone and there is also a baby-listening service. On the terrace is a superb heated swimming pool fringed by palm trees and for indoor diversion there is a pool room with table tennis and amusements. Golf, riding, watersports and fishing trips are all available near at hand. Sharpitor National Trust and Overbecks Gardens with its famous subtropical plants adjoins the hotel and the walks along the clifftops are breathtaking in their natural beauty and wildlife. 👑 👑 👑 👑, *AA***, RAC Hospitality and Service Award.*

SIDMOUNT HOTEL,
Station Road, Sidmouth,
Devon EX10 8XJ

Tel: 0395 513432*

Residential and restaurant licence; 15 bedrooms, all with private bathrooms; Historic interest; Car park (16); Lyme Regis 17 miles, Exeter 15; £/££.

A fine Georgian hotel of character in a quiet position set in two acres of beautiful gardens which contain over 300 different varieties of trees and shrubs. The hotel commands superb sea and country views of the Devonshire landscape. All bedrooms have private bathrooms and are well equipped, with colour television and tea/coffee making facilities. A central feature of the hotel is a splendid oak staircase which leads to the bedrooms. The hotel offers a high standard of comfort and excellent food. Colour brochure available on request. 🌷 🌷 🌷.

PRINCE HALL HOTEL,
Two Bridges, Yelverton,
Devon PL20 6SA

Tel: 082-289 403/4
Fax: 082-289 676

Restaurant and residential licence; 8 bedrooms, all with private bathrooms; Historic interest; Dogs welcome; Car park (15); Tavistock 8 miles, Yelverton 7; DB&B £££.

The Prince Hall Hotel is a small, friendly and relaxed country house hotel, in a peaceful and secluded setting, commanding glorious views over open moorland. All bedrooms are en suite; some have four-poster beds. The hotel offers gourmet cooking by the French owner-chef, walks from the hotel, fishing, riding and golf all close by. *ETB* 🌷 🌷 🌷 *Commended, AA and RAC**, Ashley Courtenay and Johansens Recommended.*

> * The appearance of an asterisk after the telephone number indicates that the hotel in question is closed for a period during the winter months. Exact dates should be ascertained from the hotel itself.

Dorset

ANVIL HOTEL,
Salisbury Road, Pimperne, Blandford,
Dorset DT11 8UQ
Tel: 0258 453431/480182

Fully licensed free house; 9 bedrooms, all with private bathrooms; Historic interest; Children and pets welcome; Car park (30); London 107 miles, Salisbury 24, Bournemouth 26, Poole 16; ££.

A long, low, thatched building set in a tiny village deep in the Dorset countryside — what could be more English? And that is what visitors to the Anvil will find — a typical old English hostelry offering good, old-fashioned English hospitality. A full à la carte menu is available in the charming beamed and flagged restaurant, and a wide selection of bar meals in the attractive, fully licensed bar. All bedrooms have private facilities. Ample parking. Clay pigeon shooting and tuition for individuals or parties given. Day trips in Range Rover for parties up to four. 🌂 🌂 🌂 *Commended, RAC and AA**, Good Food Pub Guide.*

The **£** symbol when appearing at the end of the italic section of an entry shows the anticipated price, during 1993, for a **single room with English Breakfast.**

Under £30	**£**	**Over £45 but under £60**	**£££**
Over £30 but under £45	**££**	**Over £60**	**££££**

This is meant as an indication only and does not show prices for Special Breaks, Weekends, etc. Guests are therefore advised to verify all prices on enquiring or booking.

KEMPS COUNTRY HOUSE HOTEL,
East Stoke, Wareham,
Dorset BH20 6AL

Tel: 0929 462563

Residential licence; 15 bedrooms, 14 with private bathrooms; Historic interest; Children welcome; Car park (26); Dorchester 17 miles, Poole 10; £££/££££.

Originally built as a Victorian Rectory, Kemps is situated in its own grounds rising from the valley of the River Frome, with lovely views of the Purbeck hills. The Victorian atmosphere is faithfully preserved and the spacious new bedrooms are pristine and tastefully decorated. There is a four poster bed in the honeymoon suite and some bedrooms have whirlpool baths. The attractive dining room has been enhanced by the addition of a Victorian conservatory extension which overlooks the garden and hills. Kemps Restaurant is Egon Ronay recommended and is well known for imaginative cooking using fresh produce; fresh bread is baked daily. All year bargain breaks. ♛ ♛ ♛ *Commended.* **See also Colour Advertisement p.8.**

ALEXANDRA HOTEL,
Pound Street, Lyme Regis,
Dorset DT7 3HZ

Tel: 0297 442010*
Fax: 0297 443229

Fully licensed; 26 bedrooms, all with private bathrooms; Children and pets welcome; Car park; Axminster 5 miles.

Superbly furnished, this gracious 18th century house stands in lovely gardens of 1½ acres from which it is only a short stroll through the Langmoor Gardens to the sea-front and famous Cobb. Not only do the guest rooms delight the eye but they are equipped with such amenities as colour television, hairdryers, radio, direct-dial telephone, baby listening intercom and tea and coffee making facility, whilst private bathrooms are standard. Three of the bedrooms are on the ground floor. Nearby, the reception area opens into a popular bar and a lounge where a fire augments central heating on cool evenings. The table d'hôte and à la carte dinners are of high standard and lunchtime bar meals and cream teas may be enjoyed in an attractive sun lounge or taken in the garden. ♛ ♛ ♛ ♛ *Commended, AA***, RAC*** Merit Awards.*

KERSBROOK HOTEL AND RESTAURANT,
Pound Road, Lyme Regis,
Dorset DT7 3HX

Tel: 0297 442596*

Restaurant and residential licence; 12 bedrooms, 10 with private bathrooms; Historic interest; Children and dogs by arrangement; Car park (14); Exeter 28 miles, Axminster 5; ££.

Thatched, and standing in its own one-and-a-half acres of beautiful garden with great old-world charm, this picturesque eighteenth century Listed hotel can also boast excellent contemporary facilities to back up its friendly and efficient service. With fine views over Lyme Bay from its elevated position, the hotel stands in lovely gardens conveniently near all the amenities of this historic little resort. Guest rooms are particularly well appointed, with private bath/shower room en suite, and tea, chocolate and coffee-making facilities and fruit. Relaxation may be sought in the cocktail lounges, whilst first-rate à la carte dinners, cooked to order by our international chef, Norman Arnold, are served in an intimate pink dining room. ✿ ✿ ✿ *Highly Commended, AA**, RAC** Blue Ribbon.*

KNOLL HOUSE HOTEL,
Studland, Near Swanage,
Dorset BH19 3AZ

Tel: 092-944 251*

Restaurant and residential licence; 80 bedrooms, 56 with private bathrooms, including 30 family suites; Children and dogs welcome; Car park (100); Corfe Castle 6 miles, Sandbanks Ferry 3; Full Board £££/££££.

On the Dorset Heritage coast this delightful hotel is surrounded by National Trust land and some of the prettiest scenery in the West Country. Knoll House is an independent country house hotel under the personal management of its owners. It overlooks three miles of beach from an attractive setting in pine trees and pleasant gardens, and offers facilities for sport and relaxation that must be counted amongst the finest in the country — two hard tennis courts, a pitch and putt course and a swimming pool. The Health Spa offers a sauna, steam room, jacuzzi and other leisure pursuits. Young children are catered for in their own dining room. See advertisement inside back cover.

> * The appearance of an asterisk after the telephone number indicates that the hotel in question is closed for a period during the winter months. Exact dates should be ascertained from the hotel itself.

Durham

HELME PARK HALL COUNTRY HOUSE HOTEL,
Near Fir Tree, Bishop Auckland,
Co. Durham DL13 4NW
Tel and Fax: 0388 730970

Licensed; 10 bedrooms, all with private bathrooms; Historic interest; Children welcome; Car park (70); Darlington 17 miles, Durham 11; £££.

With spectacular views from its elevated site, this one-time stone farmhouse is welcoming indeed. Beyond the white-fronted facade, the welcome extends to truly fine amenities in the modern idiom. Only recently rescued from neglect and decay, the house is now fully equipped as a country hotel of high distinction and character. Public rooms are spacious and brightly decorated and guest rooms are superbly appointed with bathroom en suite, colour television, radio, direct-dial telephone and several other practicalities. The beamed bar, where light meals are available, is charming, and a french window leads to five acres of garden and woodland, the ideal setting for an evening stroll before or after dining sumptuously in a restaurant with beautifully draped mullioned windows. 🌷🌷🌷🌷 *Highly Commended, RAC*** and Award for Hospitality and Service.*

OLD MANOR HOUSE HOTEL,
The Green, West Auckland,
Co. Durham DL14 9HW

Tel: 0388 834834
Fax: 0388 833566

Fully licensed; 30 bedrooms, all with private bathrooms; Historic interest; Children and pets welcome; Car park (100); Durham 9 miles; ££.

Steeped in history, this fine old manor house has associations with the Eden family which go back to the 15th century; perhaps the best known in a long line, Anthony Eden, was born here in 1897 and went on to become Prime Minister. The house has seen peaceful and turbulent times as the years have rolled by, from being a brewery in the 13th century, to Parliamentary seizure in the 16th century during the Civil War and now in its comparatively new role as a country hotel of distinction. Many of the original features remain to fascinate the modern-day visitor, to say nothing of the tales of ghosts, murder and secret passages. A great deal of care has been employed in bringing facilities to the standards required by the guest of today without spoiling the aura of stirring days gone by. Now ideally suited to the needs of tourists and businessmen, the hotel has spacious and comfortably furnished lounges and an attractive bar in which to enjoy an aperitif before dining memorably in the charming Four Seasons Restaurant. Recommended for a romantic weekend (or longer) break, bedrooms have excellent en suite amenities, colour television, radio, telephone, hair dryer, trouser press and tea and coffee-makers and some superb rooms are available with four-posters. For conferences and special occasions, the facilities are splendid, especially the galleried Knights Hall which seats 150. ♕ ♕ ♕ ♕ *Commended.*

Key to
Tourist Board Ratings

The Crown Scheme
(England, Scotland & Wales)

Covering hotels, motels, private hotels, guesthouses, inns, bed & breakfast, farmhouses. Every Crown classified place to stay is inspected annually. *The classification:* Listed then 1-5 Crown indicates the range of facilities and services. Higher quality standards are indicated by the terms APPROVED, COMMENDED, HIGHLY COMMENDED and DELUXE.

The Key Scheme
(also operates in Scotland using a Crown symbol)

Covering self-catering in cottages, bungalows, flats, houseboats, houses, chalets, etc. Every Key classified holiday home is inspected annually. *The classification:* 1-5 Key indicates the range of facilities and equipment. Higher quality standards are indicated by the terms APPROVED, COMMENDED, HIGHLY COMMENDED and DELUXE.

The Q Scheme
(England, Scotland & Wales)

Covering holiday, caravan, chalet and camping parks. Every Q rated park is inspected annually for its quality standards. The more √ in the Q – up to 5 – the higher the standard of what is provided.

Gloucestershire

CHARLTON KINGS HOTEL,
Cheltenham,
Gloucestershire GL52 6UU

Tel: 0242 231061
Fax: 0242 241900

Restaurant and residential licence; 14 bedrooms, all with private bathrooms; Children and dogs welcome; Car park (20); Bourton-on-the-Water 12 miles, Tewkesbury 10, Winchcombe 8; £££.

The ideal venue for Cheltenham and the Cotswolds situated in an acre of garden in an area of outstanding natural beauty on the edge of town. Newly opened in 1991 after extensive refurbishment. All rooms (some reserved for non-smokers) have views of the Cotswold Hills, which are easily reached on foot — there is a footpath right alongside the hotel leading onto the famous Cotswold Way. There is plenty to do and see (our room information folder lists over 200 sights/activities), or simply watch the world go by from the conservatory. During your stay you will be tempted to try our cosy bistro offering an imaginative and varied menu. Above all, we offer a standard of service only a small hotel can provide. *ETB* 👑 👑 👑 👑 *Commended.*

OLD FARMHOUSE HOTEL,
Lower Swell, Stow-on-the-Wold,
Gloucestershire GL54 1LF

Tel: 0451 830232

Restaurant and residential licence; 14 bedrooms, 12 with private bathrooms; Historic interest; Children welcome, pets in most rooms; Car park (25); Stow-on-the-Wold 1 mile; £/££.

A sixteenth century Cotswold stone farmhouse in a peaceful hamlet, now sympathetically converted to a warm, comfortable, small hotel. It is well situated for touring, exploring and sound sleeping, and has the relaxed and informal air of its farmhouse origins. The resident owners place much emphasis on the quality of the food, and real hospitality. Breakfasts are full cooked English and a table d'hôte menu is available in the evening. Vegetarians are welcome. Colour television, radio/alarm, mini-safe, telephone and tea/coffee making facilities are in all bedrooms (including two four-posters). Centrally heated throughout, with log fires. Secluded walled garden and ample private parking. Special Short Break terms throughout the year. *ETB* ✿ ✿ ✿*, AA**, Good Hotel Guide, Egon Ronay.*

PARKEND HOUSE HOTEL,
Parkend, Near Lydney,
Gloucestershire GL15 4HL

Tel: 0594 563666
Fax: 0594 564631

Residential and restaurant licence; 8 bedrooms, all with private bathrooms; Children and pets welcome; Car park (25); Lydney 4 miles; £.

We found the Royal Forest of Dean a fascinating place to visit. This is a walker's paradise in the land of the mighty oak, beech and chestnut. Until the 1960's coal in some quantity was mined here. Now the tips are grassed over although the industrial archaeologist may still seek and find the courses of old railways and tramroads. Offering first-class accommodation and food, Parkend House is a small and hospitable country house built some 200 years ago, set in three acres of parkland and boasting well-equipped and comfortable guest rooms with en suite amenities. The restaurant menu offers a good choice of English and Continental dishes and there are sporting facilities galore to promote a hearty appetite. *Les Routiers.*

THREE WAYS HOTEL,
Mickleton, Near Chipping Campden, Gloucestershire GL55 6SB

Tel: 0386 438429
Fax: 0386 438118

Licensed; 40 bedrooms, all with en suite facilities; Children and pets welcome; Car park (30); Stratford-upon-Avon 10 miles, Chipping Campden 3; £.

Superb cuisine, delightful accommodation and friendly, efficient staff, a perfect combination which makes a stay at Three Ways Hotel, home of the "Pudding Club", so enjoyable. The comfortable bedrooms with telephone, colour television, radio and tea/coffee makers are just right for either a short stay or a longer holiday, and candlelit dinners with live music on a Saturday night add the finishing touch. The hotel makes an ideal base for touring the Cotswolds and Shakespeare country and there are lovely walks in the vicinity. 🌷 🌷 🌷 🌷, *AA and RAC***.*

SEVERN BANK,
Minsterworth, Near Gloucester, Gloucestershire GL2 8JH

Tel and Fax: 0452 750357

Unlicensed; 6 bedrooms, 4 with private bathrooms; Children welcome; Car park (12); Gloucester 4 miles; £.

Severn Bank is a fine country house standing in six acres of grounds on the banks of the Severn, four miles west of Gloucester. It is ideally situated for touring the Cotswolds, the Forest of Dean and the Wye Valley, and is the recommended viewpoint for the Severn Bore tidal wave. It has a friendly atmosphere and comfortable rooms with superb views and full central heating. The en suite, non-smoking bedrooms have tea and coffee making facilities and colour television. Ample parking. 🌷 🌷 🌷, *RAC Highly Acclaimed.*

THE OLD COURT,
Newent, Gloucestershire

Tel: 0531 820522

Restaurant licence; 5 bedrooms, 2 with private bathrooms; Historic interest; Children and pets welcome; Car park (20); Gloucester 8 miles; £.

The Old Court is a magnificent William and Mary house set in its own mature walled gardens of over an acre. The old market town of Newent is close to the Wye Valley, the Cotswolds and the Forest of Dean. All bedrooms are large and comfortable, with colour television and tea and coffee making facilities; several rooms are en suite. An interesting range of traditional and Continental cuisine is served in the popular restaurant, using much local produce. There is a wide selection of fine wines. Several golf courses are nearby, as well as the famous Falconry Centre, vineyards, Butterfly Centre, National Waterways Museum, and many other places of interest. **See also Colour Advertisement p.8.**

WYCK HILL HOUSE HOTEL,
Burford Road, Stow-on-the-Wold,
Gloucestershire GL54 1HY

Tel: 0451 831936
Fax: 0451 832243

Fully licensed; 30 bedrooms, all with private bathrooms; Children welcome, pets not allowed in public rooms; Car park (70); Cheltenham 18 miles, Chipping Norton 9; ££££.

Built in mellow Cotswold stone and lying back from the road in 100 acres of landscaped gardens, this imposing manor house is elegance personified. Highlighted by rich but tasteful furnishings, the house has many architectural delights, including the gracious galleried staircase, library and sumptuously appointed bedrooms, all of which are attractively designed and equipped with bath and shower, direct-dial telephone, remote-control television and a number of thoughtful extras. Some rooms are available with four-poster or kingsize beds and those in the Coach House and Orangery annexes offer seclusion and every modern comfort. One of the most charming features of the hotel is the luxurious dining room where the superb international, award-winning cuisine has acquired a peerless reputation. *HETB* 👑 👑 👑 👑 *De Luxe, AA 2 Rosettes, Egon Ronay.*

CALCOT MANOR,
Near Tetbury,
Gloucestershire GL8 8YJ

Tel: 0666 890391
Fax: 0666 890394

Residential and restaurant licence; 15 bedrooms, all with private bathrooms; Historic interest; Children over 8 years welcome; Car park (50); Cirencester 10 miles, ££££.

The numerous special breaks organised at this historic building in the heart of the Cotswolds are a revelation. Using the hotel as a midway 'home base', one may walk the 100-mile Cotswold Way, go ballooning and gliding, tour the countryside by bicycle, go horse racing or even spend a day with the chef in the manor's kitchen, learning the secrets of the magnificent cuisine. What a delightful and well-run retreat this is with prettily decorated bedrooms, all with en suite amenities; and for that special occasion, the Master Bedroom has an exquisitely canopied and draped four-poster bed and a whirlpool bath. Active or gentle sporting diversion may be sought swimming in a sheltered and heated outdoor pool, playing croquet and with golf, riding and fishing available nearby. *AA***, Good Hotel Guide.*

TEWKESBURY PARK HOTEL, GOLF AND COUNTRY CLUB,

Lincoln Green Lane, Tewkesbury,   Tel: 0684 295405

Gloucestershire GL20 6EE   Fax: 0684 292386

Fully licensed; 78 bedrooms, all with private bathrooms; Historic interest; Children welcome; Car park (200); Gloucester 10 miles, Cheltenham 9; ££££.

Supreme comfort and care awaits guests to Tewkesbury Park, 176 acres of picturesque parkland which surround a magnificent 18th century country house which, in company with a newly added wing, provides spacious, well-planned accommodation with a full range of modern amenities and leisure opportunities that include a fine 18-hole golf course, 6-hole par 3 course, covered practice area, golf shop, club and buggy hire and professional tuition. In addition, there is an indoor heated swimming pool, squash and tennis courts, fitness studio and the option to take it easy in a health and beauty salon, sauna, solarium and steam room. This elegant and hospitable mansion also boasts the well-regarded Garden Restaurant with its mouth-watering selection of à la carte and table d'hôte dishes. Several purpose-equipped meeting rooms are available for conferences and special occasions. *HETB* 👑 👑 👑 👑 👑.

Hampshire

BOTLEY PARK HOTEL AND COUNTRY CLUB,

Winchester Road, Boorley Green, Botley,   Tel: 0489 780888

Hampshire SO3 2UA   Fax: 0489 789242

Fully licensed; 100 bedrooms, all with private bathrooms; Children welcome, pets by arrangement; Car park (250); Southampton 6 miles; ££££.

Nestling in beautiful countryside to the east of Southampton, this fine hotel features luxurious bedrooms, all with private bathrooms, as well as an extensive indoor leisure club, 18-hole golf course, tennis courts and the magnificent Winchester Restaurant where splendid à la carte dishes may be fully appreciated in delightful surroundings. Style, quality and impeccable service form the character and appeal of this excellent and elegant retreat which, although enjoying a peaceful situation, is so easy of access. Other sporting activities available include squash, tennis, snooker, an indoor swimming pool, croquet, putting and an exercise and aerobics suite. Facilities for conferences and private functions are also impressive and for residential business packages, all the amenities of the leisure club are included. *STB* 👑 👑 👑 👑 👑, *AA **** and Rosette.*

WHITLEY RIDGE COUNTRY HOUSE HOTEL,
Beaulieu Road, Brockenhurst,
Hampshire SO42 7QL

Tel: 0590 22354
Fax: 0590 22856

Residential and restaurant licence; 11 bedrooms, all with private bathrooms; Historic interest; Children and pets welcome; Car park (30); Lyndhurst 4 miles, Lymington 4; ££/£££.

Whitley Ridge is a beautiful Georgian country house hotel set in spacious grounds surrounded by the New Forest. Ponies and deer can be seen from the hotel and there is direct access into the Forest. The charming bedrooms include a four-poster, Georgian and Coronet rooms, and all are very well appointed with private facilities, television and telephone. Imaginative and reasonably priced dishes are served in the candlelit dining room where a log fire burns on cooler evenings. A cosy bar and charming drawing room are adjacent. Turn off the A337 before entering or on leaving Brockenhurst and look for the sign of the two acorns beside the B3055 road to Beaulieu. Go up the drive to this old Hunting Lodge set well away from the road. *ETB* 🌑 🌑 🌑 🌑 *Highly Commended. AA** and Rosette, Ashley Courtenay Recommended.*

CLOUD HOTEL,
Meerut Road, Brockenhurst,
Hampshire SO42 7TD

Tel: 0590 22165*

Residential licence; 19 bedrooms, 5 with private bathrooms; Children and pets welcome; Car park (20); Ringwood 11 miles, Lyndhurst 4; ££.

A tranquil retreat in the heart of the New Forest, this splendid hotel revels in its sylvan setting, yet the centre of the pretty village of Brockenhurst is only a stroll away. Family parties are really welcome here and for children under 16 there are special rates providing they are sharing with adults. A special children's tea is served from 5–5.30 p.m. High-chairs and also cots are provided. Public and guest rooms are of attractive decor and there are four comfortable lounges, including one with a bar and one with colour television. Central heating combines with the cheer of log fires to thwart winter chill. The cuisine represents home cooking at its best, the sweet trolley being a well-appreciated speciality. Small functions are also well catered for. *SETB* 🌑, *, *Ashley Courtenay.*

NEWTOWN HOUSE HOTEL,
Manor Road, Hayling Island,
Hampshire PO11 0QR

Tel: 0705 466131
Fax: 0705 461366

Fully licensed; 26 bedrooms, all with private bathrooms; Historic interest; Children and pets welcome; Car park (40); Chichester 14 miles; ££.

Spick and span and attractively furnished, Newtown House belies its somewhat gaunt Edwardian appearance, old ships' beams, oak panelling, inglenook seating and stone fireplaces all contributing to an effective old-world atmosphere: yet the amenities are of a high contemporary standard, all guest rooms blessed with baths or showers en suite, colour television, radio, telephone, tea and coffee-making facilities and hair dryers. The magnificent New Wave Leisure Complex provides a heated swimming pool, multi-gym, jacuzzi, solarium and sauna, whilst tennis and swimming tuition by a resident instructor is available. Within the hotel's lawned grounds is a fine hard tennis court and children's play area. One of the hotel's proudest features is its renowned restaurant, excellent and interesting cuisine being enhanced by friendly and efficient service. *STB* 👑 👑 👑, *Ashley Courtenay Highly Recommended.*

LITTLE FOREST LODGE,
New Forest, Ringwood,
Hampshire BH24 3HS

Tel: 0425 478848

Licensed; 5 bedrooms, all en suite; Historic interest; Children and dogs welcome; Car park (10); Salisbury 12 miles, Bournemouth 9, Lyndhurst 8; ££.

Built as a gentleman's country residence at the turn of the century, the oak-built house is elegantly furnished, with all bedrooms offering individual decor, television and tea and coffee making facilities. A full English breakfast is served in the oak-panelled dining room, with home cooking a speciality. The bar is situated in the spacious lounge leading out into the garden. The house is surrounded by three acres of landscaped gardens where delicious cream teas are served in summer months. Being only 200 yards from the New Forest, a short walk can take you to a beautiful location where you can meet the New Forest ponies and perhaps see deer roaming. We are ideally located for visiting several famous country houses, including Broadlands, Beaulieu, and Wilton House, all only a short drive away. *ETB* 👑 👑 👑, *AA Selected.*

EVERGREENS HOTEL,
Romsey Road, Lyndhurst,
Hampshire SO43 7AR

Tel: 0703 282175

Residential and restaurant licence; 19 bedrooms, all with private shower/bathrooms; Historic interest; Children and dogs welcome; Car park; London 83 miles, Salisbury 19; ££.

This country house hotel is situated in an acre of lovely gardens close to the centre of Lyndhurst, capital of the New Forest. It is personally run under new management and guests can therefore expect good food and the best of attention to their requirements in a very friendly atmosphere. Amenities include bedrooms with private shower and toilet, colour television, telephone, tea/coffee facilities; sitting room, a cosy bar with a log fire, and an excellent restaurant featuring a variety of English and Continental dishes. Come and let us spoil you.

STRING OF HORSES,
Mead End, Sway, Lymington,
Hampshire SO41 6EH

Tel: 0590 682631

Residential and restaurant licence; 8 bedrooms, all with private facilities; Car park (20); Bournemouth 15 miles, Southampton 15; ££/£££.

Unique, secluded, exclusive hotel set in four acres in the heart of the New Forest, with a friendly, relaxed atmosphere. Eight luxurious double bedrooms are available, each with its own fantasy bathroom with spa bath and shower. Every facility is offered, including colour television, direct-dial telephone, radio and tea-making facilities. Four-poster rooms are also available, making this an ideal honeymoon setting. Dine in our intimate candlelit "Carriages" restaurant. For relaxation there is a heated outdoor swimming pool. This is superb riding country, and the hotel is close to excellent yachting resorts and several good golf courses. *ETB* ❦ ❦ ❦ ❦ *Highly Commended, AA** Rosette.* **See also Colour Advertisement p.9.**

WOODLANDS LODGE HOTEL,
Bartley Road, Ashurst, Woodlands,
Hampshire SO4 2GN

Tel: 0703 292257
Fax: 0703 293090

Licensed; 16 luxury bedrooms and suites, all with private bathrooms; Historic interest; Dogs and horses welcome by arrangement; Totton 3 miles; ££££.

This beautiful Georgian building, originally a Royal hunting lodge, has been extensively renovated and refurbished to offer the highest standards of luxury and comfort, while retaining the welcoming, informal atmosphere the hotel has always enjoyed. All of the individually designed bedrooms are en suite (all with whirlpool baths), and have remote-control colour television, direct-dial telephone, trouser press etc; the spacious suites have the additional luxury of a fully furnished sitting room. Set in its own grounds in the heart of the New Forest, Woodlands Lodge is ideal for walking or riding, and stabling is available for those who wish to bring their own horses. **See also Colour Advertisement p.9.**

Herefordshire

GLEWSTONE COURT,
Glewstone, Ross-on-Wye,
Herefordshire HR9 6AW

Tel: 0989 770367
Fax: 0989 770282

Licensed; 7 bedrooms, all with private bathrooms; Historic interest; Children and pets welcome; Car park (24); Gloucester 17 miles; ££/£££.

Christine and William Reeve-Tucker fell in love with this 250-year-old manor in 1987. Set prettily in grounds and gardens surrounded by fruit orchards, it is now their family home and charming country house hotel, where informal service and warm hospitality ensure that guests really do feel like guests. The bedrooms are spacious, and tasteful furnishings throughout provide comfort while complementing the character of the house. An imaginative menu using seasonal local produce is offered in the popular restaurant. Christine is a keen balloonist, and among other activities, adventurous guests can arrange a balloon flight from the grounds. *ETB ❀ ❀ ❀ ❀ Highly Commended, AA**, Which Hotel Guide Commended, Tourist Board Award Winner, Johansens, Logis of Great Britain.*

PENCRAIG COURT HOTEL AND RESTAURANT,
Pencraig, Near Ross-on-Wye,
Herefordshire HR9 6HR

Tel: 0989 770306*

Residential and restaurant licence; 11 bedrooms, all with private bathrooms; Historic interest; Children welcome; Car park (25); Ross-on-Wye 4 miles; DB&B ££.

Standing high above the banks of the River Wye, Pencraig Court Hotel proudly surveys the beautiful countryside of this serene part of rural England. Constructed nearly 200 years ago, the hotel retains the elegance and furnishings of the Georgian era, but has been sympathetically updated so that all bedrooms now have private bath, colour television, direct-dial telephone and tea/coffee making facilities. One such room also has a four-poster bed. Duncan Sykes has run the hotel since 1973. In the hotel restaurant guests can enjoy the very best in English and French cuisine and sample a fine selection of inexpensive and interesting wines from our cellar. Free colour brochure on request. *ETB ❀ ❀ ❀, AA and RAC**.*

PENGETHLEY MANOR HOTEL,
Near Ross-on-Wye,
Herefordshire HR9 6LL

Tel: 098-987 211
Fax: 098-987 238

Fully licensed; 24 bedrooms, all with private bathrooms; Historic interest; Children and pets welcome; Car park (70); Ross-on-Wye 4 miles; ££££.

15 acres of well-tended parkland and lawns, incorporating a challenging 9-hole pitch-and-putt course, croquet lawn and trout lake, form the tranquil setting of this lovely Georgian manor house where character, style and elegance are watchwords by which this recommended retreat prospers. Hospitality and informality will endear Pengethley to family parties, for the young and not-so-young are cared for with equal attention. There are numerous amenities provided to meet the needs of children and special facilities are on hand for disabled guests. Light and airy bedrooms are beautifully furnished in a manner reminiscent of the standards of an effete bygone age, to which such contemporary practicalities as bathrooms en suite, colour television, direct-dial telephone and hair-dryers have been added. Rooms with four-poster and canopied beds are also available. The imaginative cuisine has achieved a reputation for its excellence and generosity with such delicacies as Wye salmon, prime Hereford beef and tender Welsh lamb featuring regularly in company with home-grown produce. The surrounding countryside is ideal for walking or exploring numerous places of historic interest and sporting venues whilst, alternatively, evenings 'at home' may be spent relaxing with a novel before a log fire in the panelled library or playing a few frames in the snooker room. Understandably, Pengethley is also in great demand for conferences, receptions, etc. 🌸 🌸 🌸 🌸, *AA ****.

THE STEPPES COUNTRY HOUSE HOTEL,
Ullingswick, Near Hereford,
Herefordshire HR1 3JG

Tel: 0432 820424

Residential licence; 6 bedrooms, all with private bathrooms; Historic interest; Children over 12 years and dogs welcome; Car park (6); Hereford 8 miles; DB&B ££.

Sometimes the traveller has to wander off the beaten track to find something truly original, and "The Steppes", peacefully resting in the tiny Wye Valley hamlet of Ullingswick, will more than repay those who visit it. This charming creeper-clad country hotel is furnished and decorated entirely in keeping with its seventeenth-century character. Beamed en suite bedrooms are located in a restored courtyard barn and stable, and are complete with television, clock/radio, tea/coffee making facilities and mini-bar. The cordon bleu cuisine is personally prepared by Mrs Tricia Howland, for whom each dinner served is a special occasion, appealing particularly to those with more adventurous tastes, and deserving of the best locally grown vegetables, home-baked bread, and eggs from the hotel's own hens. And what better, after an ample breakfast, than to tour the area's ancient villages, walk in the Black Mountains and Malvern Hills, visit the porcelain works in Worcester or a local cider mill. See also our advertisement on the Outside Back Cover. 🌸 🌸 🌸 🌸 *Highly Commended.*

Hertfordshire

BEDFORD ARMS THISTLE HOTEL,
Chenies, Near Rickmansworth,
Hertfordshire WD3 6EQ

Tel: 0923 283301

Fax: 0923 284825

Licensed; 10 bedrooms, all with private bathrooms; Children welcome; Car park (120); London 20 miles, Rickmansworth 4.

This small and immensely charming hotel lies on the outskirts of the attractive and historic village of Chenies, only 20 miles from Central London and easily accessible from all parts of the country via the motorway network. Warmth, tranquillity, personal attention and superb cuisine are the hallmarks of this classic English country house hotel which is set in carefully tended gardens, ideal for relaxation in fine weather. Excellent international cuisine is offered in the oak-panelled restaurant, while the lounge bar serves snacks in pleasant and informal surroundings. The deluxe bedrooms provide every comfort, including en suite bathroom, television, radio, direct-dial telephone and hairdryer; 24-hour room service is available.

PENDLEY MANOR HOTEL,
Cow Lane, Tring,
Hertfordshire HP23 5QY

Tel: 0442 891891
Fax: 0442 890687

Fully licensed; 71 bedrooms, all with private bathrooms; Historic interest; Children and pets welcome; Car park (150); London 32 miles; ££££.

Constructed in 1876 on the ruins of a 15th century Tudor manor and until recently a private residence, thoughtful refurbishment restored this elegant Victorian house to its former glory prior to its opening as an independent hotel in 1990. The opulent evidence of a bygone era, to which the most up-to-date appointments have been added, now captivates guests seeking peace, comfort and good food in gracious surroundings and its situation, so conveniently placed for London, is an added attraction, not only for tourists but also those seeking first-rate conference and function facilities. The hotel hosts an annual open air Festival each August with orchestral nights and performances of Shakespeare. The grounds comprise 35 acres of wooded parkland in which to stroll or play tennis. Exuding a warmth of welcome (augmented by blazing log fires in winter), the house has many splendid architectural features, including a suspended staircase and whispering gallery. Luxurious and spacious bedrooms and suites are tastefully decorated in harmonious colour schemes to complement such appointments as en suite bathrooms, colour television, telephone and several useful extras. Prepared by talented chefs, the magnificent, primarily English and European, cuisine is backed by a choice selection of wines. ✿ ✿ ✿ ✿ *Highly Commended, AA* ****.

Isle of Wight

SENTRY MEAD HOTEL,
Madeira Road, Totland Bay,
Isle of Wight PO39 0BJ

Tel: 0983 753212

Restaurant and residential licence; 14 bedrooms, all with private bathroom or shower room; Children and pets welcome; Car park (12); Yarmouth 3 miles; £.

Those who would like to really "get away from it all" and relax in peaceful, unspoiled surroundings are well advised to take the short trip across the Solent to the delightful Isle of Wight, where Mike and Julie Hodgson provide a friendly and comfortable haven at Sentry Mead. Set in spacious gardens, the hotel is a mere two minutes from a sandy beach and is ideally placed for exploring this lovely holiday island. The light and airy bedrooms all have en suite bathrooms or shower rooms, colour television, and radio/baby alarm; both dining room and lounge have access to the garden room and terrace, with wonderful views over the spectacular coastline. Delicious table d'hôte dinners are available in the evenings, and an interesting bar menu caters for lunchtime appetites. All in all, a truly first-rate establishment. *STB* ✿ ✿ ✿, *AA**, Ashley Courtenay, Les Routiers.* **See also Colour Advertisement p.10.**

Kent

EASTWELL MANOR HOTEL,
Eastwell Park, Boughton Lees, Ashford,
Kent TN25 4HR

Tel: 0233 635751
Fax: 0233 635530

Fully licensed; 23 bedrooms, all with en suite facilities; Historic interest; Children welcome, pets by arrangement; Car park (200); Folkestone 16 miles, Canterbury 14, Ashford 3; ££££.

This lovingly restored country house hotel and restaurant, standing in 62 acres of grounds in private parkland, was rebuilt from the ground in 1926, although the original manor dates back to 1069. Fresh flowers and cheerful log fires provide a warm welcome all year round. The bedrooms are individually furnished to a very high standard, with private bathroom and shower, colour television, radio and trouser press. The elegant wood-panelled dining room offers excellent cuisine matched by a well balanced wine list and attentive service. Falconry, hot air ballooning, tennis and croquet can be enjoyed within the grounds, and activities such as golf, squash, horse riding and fishing can be arranged locally. *SEETB* 🏵 🏵 🏵 🏵 🏵 *De Luxe, AA 4 Red Stars, RAC 4 Stars, Egon Ronay, Good Food Guide, "County Restaurant of the Year" 1991.*

ABBOTS BARTON HOTEL,
New Dover Road, Canterbury,
Kent

Tel: 0227 760341
Fax: 0797 226995

Fully licensed; 42 bedrooms, all with private bathrooms; Historic interest; Children welcome; Car park (80); London 58 miles, Dover 15; ££.

A true country house hotel only a few minutes' walk from the City Walls and Cathedral, Abbots Barton is set in two acres of gardens. Built on the Barley Farm of St. Augustine and having served the citizens of Canterbury for over 150 years, it has now achieved fame and favour as a first-class hotel with superb, skilfully introduced modern facilities. With an historic theme which recalls Chaucer's 'Canterbury Tales', bedrooms have private bathrooms, colour television, radio and direct-dial telephone, whilst suites and four-posters are also available. The restaurant, specialising in local produce, is well regarded for its excellent cuisine and there are several impressive conference and function rooms, including the Cathedral Room which seats over 100 guests. 🏵 🏵 🏵 🏵 *Approved, AA**.*

WOODPECKERS COUNTRY HOTEL,
Womenswold, Near Canterbury,
Kent
Tel: 0227 831319

Residential and restaurant licence; 15 bedrooms, 6 with private bathrooms; Dover 9 miles, Canterbury 7; £.

A really first-rate country holiday venue for families, this former rectory presents the most helpful amenities for parents and their charges. Throughout there is a friendly and informal atmosphere to which the young, in particular, will instantly respond. Bedrooms include a four-poster, one with a brass bedstead, Georgian and bridal bedrooms, all en suite and with colour television and tea/coffee making facilities. There are two comfortable lounges, one with television and a selection of children's games, and a luxury bar. The grounds extend to two acres, and incorporate a heated swimming pool, swing, slide, sandpit and pets corner. Extremely popular with guests of all ages is the excellent traditional English cuisine, served by a willing staff under the kindly supervision of proprietors Pat and Ted Millard.

THE OLD CLOTH HALL,
Cranbrook,
Kent TN17 3NR
Tel: 0580 712220*

Unlicensed; 3 bedrooms, all with private bathrooms; Historic interest; Car park; Tenterden 7 miles; £££.

Once visited by Queen Elizabeth I, this charming, timbered house dates from the 15th century and stands in 13 acres of lovely gardens with magnificent rhododendrons and azaleas. There is a sheltered swimming pool and hard tennis court. Inside, the house is fascinating with beams and inglenook log fires underlining its time-honoured appeal. With London, the south coast and many places of historic and sporting interest within easy reach, this is a popular and tranquil holiday retreat and the facilities for guests are of a very high standard. *Derek Johansen Award for Excellence 1991.*

ST. MARGARET'S HOTEL AND COUNTRY CLUB,
Reach Road, St. Margaret-at-Cliffe, Dover, Kent CT15 6AE

Tel: 0304 853262
Fax: 0304 853434

Licensed; 24 bedrooms, all with private bathrooms; Children welcome, guide dogs only; Car park (100); Dover 4 miles; ££.

A fine modern complex including a country club and fitness centre, this is an inspired holiday venue with the requirements of every member of the family borne in mind all year round. Modern double and twin-bedded rooms offer the very latest in comfort with bathrooms en suite, television, telephone and tea-making facilities, whilst the restaurant has a reputation for superb home cooking. The day starts with the option of a full English breakfast or the lighter Continental variety and lunchtime (and evening) snacks are served in either of two bars. The atmosphere is informal and there are countless activities to enjoy; heated indoor swimming pools, a large family pool and a superb exercise pool for the serious swimmer, a fully-equipped gymnasium, sauna, solarium, tennis courts and much more. Never a dull moment! For children there is a special activity play area and opportunities for instruction in swimming, scuba diving or canoeing. And for the body conscious, osteopathy, massage and beauty therapies are available. High on the cliffs above the bay, St. Margaret's lies between the historic ports of Dover and Deal and is surrounded by National Trust land. There are many outdoor pursuits to be enjoyed in the area as well as numerous places of historic interest. *SEETB* 🏵 🏵 🏵.

TUDOR COURT HOTEL,
Hawkhurst, Kent

Tel: 0580 752312
Fax: 0580 753966 Telex: 957565 TCH

Licensed; 20 bedrooms, all with private bathrooms; Historic interest; Children welcome; Car park (60); Maidstone 17 miles, Hastings 15, Rye 13; £££.

A charming hotel with a country atmosphere, the Tudor Court is a warm and friendly, well-run establishment with a restaurant that is open to non-residents. Here is the setting for imaginative and well-planned dishes, all skilfully prepared by an experienced chef who enjoys cooking with locally grown produce. The hotel's extensive grounds, which include a children's play area, are well kept and have shaded lawns and colourful flower beds. The lovely Weald of Kent invites closer acquaintance on all sides, and jaunts to the coast may be made by way of variety. Bedrooms are well appointed, with private bathroom, direct-dial telephone, radio, colour television, trouser press and teasmade. There are two bars as well as a sunny lounge. A colour brochure and tariff are available on request. *ETB* 🏵 🏵 🏵 🏵, *AA and RAC**.*

COLLINA HOUSE HOTEL,
East Hill, Tenterden,
Kent TN30 6RL

Tel: 05806 4852

Licensed; 11 bedrooms, all with private bathrooms; Children welcome, pets by arrangement only; Car park (11); Ashford 10 miles; £.

This charming hotel is quietly situated in the country town of Tenterden, yet is only a few minutes' walk from the Leisure Centre. There are many National Trust properties and places of interest in the area, including Sissinghurst Castle, Leeds Castle, Scotney Castle Gardens and the Kent and East Sussex steam engines. Personal attention is assured by the Swiss-trained owners of this comfortable hotel, who provide home cooking of the highest standard, enhanced by the use of home-grown produce. All the well-appointed bedrooms, including five family rooms, have private bathrooms, central heating and colour television. Further details on request. 🌷 🌷 🌷.

Lancashire

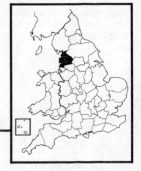

HARROP FOLD COUNTRY FARMHOUSE HOTEL,
Bolton-by-Bowland,
Lancashire BB7 4PJ

Tel: 020-07 600*

Residential licence; 8 bedrooms, all with private bathrooms; Historic interest; Car park (10); Gisburn 3 miles; £££.

A truly 'hideaway' country retreat, this superbly modernised character farmhouse nestles in 280 acres in a secluded valley amidst twisting lanes, sparkling streams and rolling green fields. Of Viking origin and fortified by local stone around the 17th century, the house is sturdily built with mullioned windows. Here is escape to a world of real values orchestrated by the Wood family. A bottle of wine awaits you on arrival within the superb en suite bedrooms which are named and co-ordinated to correspond with local wild flowers. The house is delightfully decorated with horse brasses, oak beams and antiques creating a warm and relaxing atmosphere whilst dining in style on excellent farmhouse fare is an unforgettable experience. *NWTB* 🌷 🌷 🌷 🌷 *Commended, AA Selected, RAC Acclaimed, Johansens Recommended.*

Please mention
Recommended COUNTRY HOTELS
when seeking refreshment or
accommodation at a Hotel
mentioned in these pages

THE PICKERINGS,
Garstang Road, Catterall, Garstang,
Lancashire PR3 0HA

Tel: 0995 602133

Restaurant and residential licence; 16 bedrooms (2 ground floor), all with private bathrooms; Children welcome; Car park; Blackpool 12 miles, Lancaster 10; ££.

The Pickerings is a delightful country house slightly hidden by a magnificent cedar tree in the small village of Catterall on the outskirts of the ancient market town of Garstang. An ideal base for visiting all neighbouring regions including the Fylde Coast, Trough of Bowland, Lancashire and Pendle, and the Southern Lake District. At the Pickerings the surroundings and service are for the discerning, with individually furnished lounges and bedrooms, hearty breakfasts served as late as you wish, and rich five-course dinners served until late each evening. Two acres of well-tended gardens are available for relaxation, and nearby are several golf courses, nature trails and picnic sites. Very special "Summer Holiday" bargain rates from April to September. *AA**, RAC.*

LANE HEAD,
Millhouses, Wray, Near Hornby, Lancaster,
Lancashire LA2 8NF

Tel: 05242 21148

Licensed; all bedrooms with private bathrooms; Historic interest; Lancaster 8 miles; £.

This old farmhouse in the heart of the Lune Valley is pleasantly situated off the beaten track yet by no means isolated. It is not just the location which makes Lane Head special; the house dates back to the 1700s and has been extensively renovated to provide luxury accommodation. All bedrooms are en suite and have tea/coffee making facilities, radio, television and telephone. A large oak-panelled entrance area leads to a spacious lounge, well-stocked bar, and dining room. The restaurant, which is open to the public on Thursdays, Fridays and Saturdays, has an extensive à la carte menu. There is a pond with many species of water fowl. This is an ideal base from which to tour the Dales, Lakes or coast. Regret no children or pets please. 🌷🌷🌷.

OLD MILL HOTEL,
Springwood, Ramsbottom,
Lancashire BL0 9DS

Tel: 0706 822991
Fax: 0706 822291

Fully licensed; 36 bedrooms, all with private bathrooms; Historic interest; Children welcome; Car park (100); Bury 4½ miles; ££.

Delightful gardens contribute greatly to the visual appeal of this spruce Tudor-style hotel and the appointments within are equally pleasing to the eye. Supervised by Owner, Karen Sacco, a newly-completed bedroom and luxury leisure complex has been designed and built in the style of the original building. Each bedroom is attractively equipped with bathroom en suite, remote-control television, radio alarm, direct-dial telephone and tea and coffee-making facilities amongst the thoughtful provisions. The superb leisure centre includes a swimming pool, whirlpool bath, sauna, solarium and fully-equipped gymnasium. Hearty appetites will be well satisfied, either in the chic Trattoria da Nicola with its tasty Italian dishes or in a highly acclaimed restaurant famed for its fine French and English cuisine. 🌷🌷🌷🌷🌷 Commended, ***.

THE SPREAD EAGLE HOTEL,
Sawley, Near Clitheroe,
Lancashire BB7 4NH

Tel: 0200 41202/41406

Licensed; 10 bedrooms, all with private facilities; Historic interest; Children welcome; Car park (80); Skipton 19 miles, Preston 18. ££.

The Spread Eagle Hotel lies on a picturesque bend of the River Ribble and the large picture windows afford wonderful views of the river and surrounding countryside. Its situation and good food have made it a popular meeting place for years. The bars offer a wide choice of drinks, including the well-known local ales, and a comprehensive list of wines. Renowned for its excellent cuisine and service, the hotel is open for luncheons and dinners every day. Each of the 10 bedrooms has a private bath or shower room, colour television, radio alarm, telephone, heating and tea/coffee making facilities. There are many walks, places of historic interest, golf, fishing and shooting nearby.

Lincolnshire

MOOR LODGE HOTEL,
Branston, Lincoln,
Lincolnshire LN4 1HU

Tel: 0522 791366
Fax: 0522 794389

Fully licensed; 25 bedrooms, all with private bathrooms; Children and pets welcome; Car park (150); Lincoln 4 miles; £££.

Beautifully decorated and with appointments of the very highest order, this privately-owned hotel has a rural setting, yet the ancient city of Lincoln is only three miles away along the B1188. The views of the famous cathedral, floodlit at night, are enchanting. Guest rooms come in a variety of sizes, all being superbly appointed with bathrooms en suite, direct-dial telephone, colour television, radio and tea and coffee-making facilities, plus cots for the very young. Meals chosen from appetite-inducing table d'hôte and à la carte menus are taken in the evocative Arnhem Room Restaurant, named after the Parachute Regiment who trained close by. On the same theme, the magnificent Lancaster Bar recalls the men of the Dam Busters who flew from nearby R.A.F. Scampton. Excellent amenities exist for conferences and functions. 🌸 🌸 🌸, *Egon Ronay Family Hotel, Ashley Courtenay.*

The **£** symbol when appearing at the end of the italic section of an entry shows the anticipated price, during 1993, for a **single room with English Breakfast.**

Under £30	**£**	**Over £45 but under £60**	**£££**
Over £30 but under £45	**££**	**Over £60**	**££££**

This is meant as an indication only and does not show prices for Special Breaks, Weekends, etc. Guests are therefore advised to verify all prices on enquiring or booking.

Norfolk

BUNWELL MANOR HOTEL,
**Bunwell, Near Norwich,
Norfolk NR16 1QU**

Tel: 095-378 8304*

Licensed; 10 bedrooms, all with private shower/bathrooms; Historic interest; Children and pets welcome; Car park (30); Norwich 12 miles, Diss 9; ££/£££.

Although tastefully modernised, there is ample evidence of the sixteenth century origins of this graceful house which combines charm and character with the distinctive service expected by the guest of today. Beneath the beamed ceilings, all rooms are centrally heated, attractively furnished and have their own facilities. The hotel has a warm, country feel about it and Mr and Mrs Nylk, the proprietors, take a personal interest in the welfare of their guests. The à la carte and table d'hôte menus are varied and interesting. The Tudor dining room is very distinctive and the Regency bar overlooks the garden and lawns. The hotel stands in its own grounds on the edge of a very peaceful village, but central to all the Norfolk holiday activities. Short Breaks available all year. *ETB* 🏵 🏵 🏵*, AA and RAC**.*

THE OLD RECTORY,
Gissing, Diss,
Norfolk IP22 3XB

Tel: 037-977 575
Fax: 037-977 4427

Unlicensed; 3 bedrooms, all with private facilities; Children welcome; Car park (6); Diss 5 miles; £.

This delightful Victorian house is situated five miles north of Diss and central to East Anglia. It stands in substantial grounds of mature gardens and woodland and is a haven of peace, comfort and elegance. The house is beautifully furnished and decorated. The bedrooms are large and comfortable and all have en suite or private bathrooms. Every effort has been made to ensure a memorable stay — tea and coffee making facilities, notepaper, colour television, hairdryers, fresh flowers and an extensive range of toiletries. Breakfast is copious and beautifully presented. Candlelit dinner is available by prior arrangement. Guests may use the heated indoor swimming pool, play croquet on the lawns or just relax on the terraces. Smoking restrictions. 🏵 🏵 🏵 *Highly Commended, Guestaccom Good Room Award.*

KING'S HEAD HOTEL,
Great Bircham, King's Lynn,
Norfolk PE31 6RJ

Tel: 048-523 265

Fully licensed; 5 bedrooms, all with private bathrooms, bath/shower; Historic interest; Children welcome; Car park (100); Docking 3 miles.

Situated on the edge of the Royal Sandringham Estate, the King's Head Hotel is ideally placed for a whole host of holiday activities in this beautiful, unspoilt part of Norfolk. It is close to King's Lynn and the coast, with many places of historic interest in the area as well as a wide range of sporting and leisure pursuits. The five charming bedrooms are all en suite, and have beverage-making facilities and colour television. The two friendly and comfortable bars offer a wide selection of refreshments, and there is a cosy residents' lounge and a large garden. The Lodge Restaurant boasts a wide-ranging à la carte menu, as well as daily specialities with a choice of starters, main courses and sweets, with the emphasis on fresh local produce, including seafood. 🏵 🏵 🏵.

KNIGHTS HILL HOTEL,
Knights Hill Village, South Wootton, King's Lynn,
Norfolk PE30 3HQ
Tel: 0553 675566; Fax: 0553 675568

Licensed; 54 bedrooms, all with private bathrooms; Children welcome, pets by arrangement; Car park (350); King's Lynn 2 miles; ££££.

This unique conversion of an 11-acre farm complex offers an exceptional range of facilities. A choice of differing styles of accommodation is provided by the main house, coach house or ground-floor apartments, each option being of equal merit in respect of their superb appointments. The cuisine also offers freedom of choice for one may dine memorably in either the elegant Garden Restaurant or in traditional country inn style in the hotel's own 'Farmers Arms'. Guests staying at this splendid hotel have full access to the very well equipped Health and Leisure Club with its indoor pool, jacuzzi, steam room, sauna and fitness studio. The Knights Barn Conference, Exhibition and Banqueting Centre is a popular venue for functions large or small. ✿ ✿ ✿ ✿ *Commended, AA/RAC***.*

CONGHAM HALL COUNTRY HOUSE HOTEL,
Grimston, King's Lynn,
Norfolk PE32 1AH
Tel: 0485 600250
Fax: 0485 601191

Residential and restaurant licence; 14 bedrooms, all with private bathrooms; Historic interest; Car park (50); King's Lynn 7 miles; ££££.

Guest rooms, which include a choice of four-poster rooms or suites, are delightfully furnished in period style at this warm and welcoming venue. Here, beset by beautiful parkland which extends to 40 acres, one can but be impressed with the style and elegance retained in converting this Georgian manor house into a luxury country hotel. Splendid opportunities exist here for the sportingly inclined for the hotel has its own swimming pool, tennis court, cricket pitch and stabling whilst, nearby, there are several good golf courses as well as clay-pigeon shooting and the racecourses of Newmarket and Fakenham. Activated appetites are well catered for in the attractive Orangery Restaurant where imaginative dishes add another facet to the lure of this fine retreat. ✿ ✿ ✿ ✿ *Highly Commended, AA Red Stars with 2 Rosettes, RAC *** and Blue Ribbon.*

OAKWOOD HOUSE HOTEL,
Tottenhill, King's Lynn,
Norfolk PE33 0RH
Tel: 0553 810256

Residential and restaurant licence; 10 bedrooms, 8 with private bathrooms; Historic interest; Children welcome, pets by arrangement; Car park (20); King's Lynn 6 miles; ££.

Compared with some of the multi-starred edifices that grace these pages, this picturesque Georgian house is dwarfed but it is, nevertheless, charming, elegant and supremely comfortable in all aspects of guest care. It stands in mature grounds on the A10 road a few miles south of King's Lynn. A fine centre for visits to the coast, fens, Sandringham, Ely and Cambridge, this is a warm, welcoming and relaxing place in which to stay. Guest rooms are individually furnished to a high standard and some ground-floor rooms, suitable for wheelchair access, are available in the converted stable block overlooking the gardens. There is a well-stocked bar and the excellent cuisine is wholesomely traditional with special diets and the needs of young children thoughtfully catered for. *EATB* ✿ ✿ ✿, *AA Listed, RAC Acclaimed.*

SCOLE INN,
Scole, Diss,
Norfolk IP21 4DR

Tel: 0379 740481
Fax: 0379 740762

Fully licensed; 24 bedrooms, all with private bathrooms; Historic interest; Children and pets welcome; Norwich 20 miles, Bury St Edmunds 20; DB&B ££.

The Scole Inn is a delightful, unspoilt coaching inn with a wealth of history. The individually appointed bedrooms all have full en suite facilities, and some have four-poster beds. Delicious food is served in the elegant restaurant. There are two characterful bars, with cosy inglenook log fires in winter. 🐾 🐾 🐾 🐾 *Commended.*

SOUTH WALSHAM HALL,
South Walsham, Norwich,
Norfolk NR13 6DQ

Tel: 060-549 378*
Fax: 060-549 519

Restaurant and club licence; 17 bedrooms, all with private bathrooms; Historic interest; Children welcome, pets by arrangement; Car park (50); Acle 3 miles; ££.

Deep in the heart of the unspoiled Norfolk Broads, South Walsham Hall offers comfort, relaxation and a cordial welcome to those seeking a base for exploring the famous waterways and the many other attractions of the Royal County. De luxe, superior and standard rooms are available, all with private bath or shower; delightful family rooms can also be obtained. Leisure facilities here are excellent, allowing one to test one's fitness with a lively (or leisurely!) game of tennis or squash; in the summer months a heated outdoor pool proves a great attraction. The City of Norwich has excellent road and rail links to the rest of the country, and nearby are connecting points for sailings to the Continent, making this an ideal stopover on a longer journey. 🐾 🐾 🐾 🐾, *AA ****.

Northumberland

VALLUM LODGE HOTEL,
Military Road, Twice Brewed, Near Bardon Mill, Northumberland NE47 7AN

Tel: 0434 344248

Licensed; 7 bedrooms, some en suite; Dogs by arrangement; Car park (25); Haltwhistle 3 miles; £.

Situated in open countryside close by Hadrian's Wall in Northumberland National Park, this delightful, quiet and peaceful hotel offers every comfort. All seven ground floor rooms have washbasins, radio alarms and tea-makers; some en suite. There is a residents' bar, a lounge with television and a large garden. Excellent food is freshly prepared using local produce. This is a superb walking area, and the hotel is convenient for all Roman sites and for many fine country houses. Large car park. A warm and friendly welcome awaits you. ♛♛ *Commended, AA*.*

WAREN HOUSE HOTEL,
Waren Mill, Belford, Northumberland NE70 7EE

Tel: 06684 581
Fax: 06684 484

Fully licensed; 7 bedrooms, including 2 suites, all with private bathrooms; Historic interest; Pets by arrangement; Car park (20); Coldstream 20 miles, Alnwick 15; £££.

This beautifully restored and refurbished eighteenth century country house hotel is set in six acres of wooded grounds on the edge of the Budle Bay Bird Sanctuary, two miles from the majestic Bamburgh Castle and overlooking Holy Island. Peace and tranquillity are words often used, but here at Waren House they really do apply from the moment you turn up the 200-yard drive. The entrance hall, complete with baby grand and masses of flowers, open fire, antique dolls and furniture, leads into the impressive drawing room and well-stocked library. The magnificent dining room is filled with family portraits and antique furniture, the tables set with crisp white linen, silver and crystal, the outlook over Budle Bay towards Holy Island . . . tranquillity. The quality and variety of the food is matched by the wine list of 200-plus bins. There are very few memorable traditional country house hotels, but we feel sure that once you have been to Waren House the friendliness of the staff, the quality of the food and furnishings, along with the magnificent surroundings will make you want to join the ever-growing band of friends who return time and time again. No children please. No smoking except in the library. *ETB ♛ ♛ ♛ ♛ Highly Commended, RAC*** and Merit Award for Overall Comfort, Voted Favourite "Best of Northumberland" Hotel, 1992.*

RIVERDALE HALL HOTEL AND RESTAURANT,
Bellingham, Hexham,
Northumberland NE48 2JT
Tel: 0434 220254

Licensed; 20 bedrooms, all with private bathrooms; Children and dogs welcome; Car park (60); Hexham 17 miles, Kielder Water 8; ££.

Set in Northumberland National Park, this is the nearest hotel to Kielder Water and Forest. Popular with the sporting enthusiast, Riverdale Hall has its own indoor swimming pool, games room, sauna, cricket field, and salmon and trout river, and just opposite is Bellingham's golf course. The Pennine Way and National Trust walks pass through the town, and Hadrian's Wall is nearby. The hotel is centrally heated throughout, and much character is added by log fires and four-poster beds. The restaurant has an RAC Merit Award for its high standard of cuisine. John Cocker, resident owner, is a keen sportsman and friendly host. *ETB* 👑 👑 👑.

TURRET HOUSE HOTEL,
Etal Road, Berwick-upon-Tweed,
Northumberland TD15 2EG
Tel: 0289 330808
Fax: 0289 330467

Full hotel licence; 13 bedrooms, all with private bathrooms; Historic interest; Children and pets welcome; Car park (60); Alnwick 30 miles, Coldstream 14; £££.

Historic Berwick-upon-Tweed has seen many turbulent times through the years, having been claimed and counter-claimed by the Scots and English on countless occasions. At peace now and endowed with great character, the old town stands in surroundings of outstanding natural beauty with castles, stately homes, miles of unspoilt coastline and tranquil villages to explore. Where better to stay than the hospitable Turret House, built in 1860 and recently refurbished to provide excellent accommodation, all guest rooms having private baths or showers, colour television, radio and tea and coffee-making facilities. The noteworthy dinner menu presents a choice of dishes of very high standard, a speciality being Hot Poached Tweed Salmon. The house is quietly set in 2 acres of landscaped grounds some 10 minutes' walk from the town centre. 👑 👑 👑 👑 *Commended, AA and RAC ****.

LANGLEY CASTLE HOTEL,
Langley-on-Tyne, Hexham,
Northumberland NE47 5LU

Tel: 0434 688888
Fax: 0434 684019

Residential and restaurant licence; 8 bedrooms, all with private bathrooms; Historic interest; Children and small, well-behaved pets welcome; Car park (100); Hexham 9 miles; £££.

England's only fortified castle hotel and an intriguing place in which to stay, the 14th century Langley Castle, with its 7 ft. walls, is, today, the perfect refuge from the stresses of the modern world. More practically, it is a fascinating base from which to explore the Northumbrian National Park and Hadrian's Wall, with contemporary luxuries and comforts blending easily with its time-hallowed atmosphere. The castle has seen turbulent and tranquil years slip by and now, as a first-class hotel and noted restaurant, has embarked on a new chapter in its history. Apart from its considerable architectural appeal, the castle has superbly appointed bedrooms, all individually furnished and with private bathrooms, whilst some include special amenities such as a sauna and jacuzzi. ❦❦❦❦ *Commended.*

BAMBURGH CASTLE HOTEL,
Seahouses,
Northumberland NE68 7SQ

Tel and Fax: 0665 720283

Fully licensed; 21 bedrooms, all with private bathrooms; Historic interest; Children and pets welcome; Car park (30); Alnwick 14 miles; ££.

The attractions of this fine seafront hotel vie with each other for precedence for they are all excellent in their own field. Without prejudice, we take position first — and first in its category it should be for, overlooking the harbour and with fabulous views of the Farne Islands, the hotel probably enjoys the finest setting on the Northumbrian coast. As to hospitality and accommodation, guests are presented with a complimentary glass of sherry on arrival (children get a goodie bag and can of pop) and are shown to a delightfully appointed bedroom with private facilities, colour television with satellite channels, direct-dial telephone, central heating and a host of thoughtful extras. Worthy of special mention is the most imaginative cuisine, the reasonably-priced four-course dinner menu offering a wide and appetising choice. A full range of food is also available in the bars and special dietary requests can be accommodated, preferably by prior arrangement. Comfort and relaxation come hand in hand with three attractive lounge areas and a bar playing a full part. For the actively inclined, there are exercise machines, a putting green and a golf driving net. For special occasions, the conference and function facilities are first-class. For exploration of the historic and scenic pleasures of Northumberland, there can be few finer places than this friendly and efficiently run hotel. ❦❦❦❦, *AA **, Les Routiers.*

Nottinghamshire

OLD ENGLAND HOTEL,
High Street, Sutton-on-Trent, Near Newark,
Nottinghamshire NG23 6QA
Tel: 0636 821216

Restaurant licence; 10 bedrooms, all with private facilities; Historic interest; Children and dogs welcome; Car park; London 133 miles, Nottingham 28, Newark-on-Trent 8; £££.

Appropriately named, the Old England Hotel, owned and run by the Pike family for over fifty years, epitomises traditional hospitality, charm and courtesy, together with the modern amenities we expect from a first-class establishment. All bedrooms are individually appointed, with private facilities and colour television, and the hotel is graced with a large collection of antique furniture, delightfully displayed in its old world setting. The menu too is selected from the very best of traditional fare, using locally produced meat and fresh vegetables. Extensive grounds invite the stroller, and Sherwood Forest and Southwell Minster are readily accessible.

Oxfordshire

CROWN & CUSHION HOTEL AND LEISURE CENTRE,
Chipping Norton, Near Oxford,
Freephone for brochure: 0800 585251
Oxfordshire OX7 5AD
Fax: 0608 642926

Fully licensed; 40 bedrooms, all with private bathrooms; Historic interest; Children and pets welcome; Car park (30); Oxford 20 miles; ££.

Five-hundred-year-old coaching inn, tastefully modernised to provide 40 excellent en suite bedrooms; some four-poster suites. Among its many attractions are an "old world" bar, log fires, real ale and good food. Facilities include an indoor pool, squash court, multi-gym and solarium; full size snooker table subject to availablity. There is also a fully equipped modern conference centre. The hotel is located in a picturesque Cotswolds town, midway between Oxford and Stratford-upon-Avon, convenient for London, Heathrow Airport and the M40 motorway. Blenheim Palace, Warwick Castle, Broadway, Bourton-on-the-Water, Bibury, Stow-on-the-Wold and Shakespeare Country are all nearby. *ETB* 🏆 🏆 🏆 🏆 *Approved, Egon Ronay, Ashley Courtenay, Les Routiers.*

EASINGTON HOUSE HOTEL & RESTAURANT,
50 Oxford Road, Banbury,
Oxfordshire OX16 9AN

Tel: 0295 270181

Licensed; 12 bedrooms, 9 with private bathrooms; Historic interest; Car park; Oxford 20 miles, Stratford-upon-Avon 18; ££.

Just five minutes' walk from Banbury's famous Cross, this former Royal Manor farmhouse now offers modern comfort in a house of exceptional charm and friendliness. Whilst dining guests can look out onto award-winning, country house-style gardens, and during the summer (weather permitting) barbecues and breakfasts on the patio are very popular. All bedrooms plus our beautifully appointed cottage are of an extremely high standard, and guests can be assured of excellent value in all aspects of the hotel and restaurant. The latter is open to non-residents and is extremely popular with those exploring the many places of interest in the area, including Broughton Castle, Chipping Campden, Blenheim Palace and the beautiful Cherwell Valley. Banbury is an ideal touring centre, being convenient for Stratford-upon-Avon, Oxford, Warwick, Leamington Spa and the Cotswolds. 👑👑👑👑, RAC Highly Acclaimed, Les Routiers, Guestaccom, Johansens.

THE PEACOCK HOTEL,
Henton, Near Chinnor, Thame OX9 4AH

Tel: 0844 53519

Fully licensed; 20 bedrooms, all with private bathrooms; Historic interest; School-age children welcome, small dogs by arrangement; Car park (55); Thame 4 miles; £/££.

This small country hotel is situated at the foot of the Chilterns, and is ideally placed for exploring this beautiful part of the country. Traditional character combines with modern facilities and comforts, making it the perfect setting for all occasions, whether business or pleasure. All rooms have private bathrooms, colour satellite television, telephone and tea-making facilities, and some have the added luxury of four-poster beds. For extra special occasions there is an executive room with lounge area and spa bath and the Chiltern Suite. The intimate dining room offers a wide selection of superb English food with a French influence, and the cosy lounge bar is the perfect setting for a relaxing after-dinner drink. 👑👑👑👑 Commended, Johansens, Egon Ronay.

WESTWOOD COUNTRY HOTEL,
Hinksey Hill Top, Oxford,
Oxfordshire OX1 5BG

Tel: 0865 735408*
Fax: 0865 736536

Restaurant and residential licence; 27 bedrooms, all with private bathrooms; Children welcome; Car park (40); Gloucester 49 miles, Reading 26; £££.

The leafy grounds of this fine hotel are a bonus for nature lovers, for the four acres are frequented by many species of birds, badgers, foxes, squirrels and even deer, and are surrounded by a further 400 acres of woodland nature reserve opened by David Bellamy. The hotel itself was discovered to be frequented by astute tourists, many of whom return to sample again the excellent accommodation and superb cuisine. Single, double and family rooms all have private facilities, television, radio, baby listening devices, and tea and coffee makers. There is a comfortable lounge with colour television and a convivial bar. Sauna, jacuzzi and mini-gym available free to guests. Good facilities exist for conferences, meetings and weddings. Short Break holidays available. AA**, Winner 1991 Daily Mail Hotel Award. **See also Colour Advertisement p.10.**

STUDLEY PRIORY HOTEL,
Horton-cum-Studley, Oxford, Oxfordshire OX33 1AZ

Tel: 086-735 203
Fax: 086-735 613

Residential licence; 19 bedrooms, all with private bathrooms; Historic interest; Children welcome; Car park (100); Oxford 6 miles; ££££.

In the 12th century a Benedictine nunnery, this fine building was converted into an hotel in 1961 and now provides splendid contemporary comforts which blend in subtle fashion with the gracious aura of unhurried days gone by. The Priory has changed little in external appearance since the days of Queen Elizabeth I and it retains its imposing presence. Log fires in the main reception room and oak panelled bar augment the central heating to provide a real warmth of welcome to present-day guests. Standing in 13 acres of wooded grounds and within easy reach of Oxford and numerous places of historic and rural interest, the hotel has exceptionally fine accommodation with en suite facilities and is also a most popular venue for conferences and functions. *AA *** and 2 Restaurant Rosettes, RAC Merit Award, Egon Ronay.*

SPRINGS HOTEL,
Wallingford Road, North Stoke, Wallingford, Oxfordshire OX10 6BE

Tel: 0491 36687
Fax: 0491 36877

Fully licensed; 38 bedrooms, all with private bathrooms; Children welcome, pets by arrangement; Car park (120); Wallingford 2 miles; ££££.

Taking its name from springs that feed a lake that graces attractive grounds of over 5 acres, this fine mock-Tudor house offers remarkable amenities indoor and out. Guest rooms are delightfully decorated and have private bathrooms, colour television, direct-dial telephone and mini-bars whilst executive suites have jacuzzi spas. Dining in the romantic atmosphere of the Fourways Restaurant is an experience to savour; the menu is imaginative and changed regularly. In the grounds, floodlit at night, is a tennis court, croquet lawn, putting green, heated swimming pool and sauna. Riding, golf and boating may be enjoyed nearby. This is a lovely place in which to unwind and it is easy to understand its popularity for conferences and functions. 👑👑👑👑 *Highly Commended, AA Rosette.*

THE WELL HOUSE,
High Street, Watlington, Oxfordshire OX9 5PY

Tel: 049-161 3333

Restaurant and residential licence; 10 bedrooms, all with private bathrooms; Historic interest; Children welcome; Car park (15); Oxford 15 miles, Henley 9; £/££.

Nestling at the foot of the Chiltern Hills and in a conservation area, yet only two miles from the M40, The Well House has been part of this attractive old village for many years — indeed part of the hotel dates from the fifteenth century. Delicious restaurant meals are served daily, both at lunchtimes and in the evenings, and bar meals are available by arrangement. The ten bedrooms are comfortably equipped and all have private bathrooms. For the active visitor squash and tennis can be arranged, and there are many delightful walks, whilst for art lovers the glories of Oxford, Stonor Park and Blenheim Palace are a short drive away. *ETB* 👑👑👑👑 *Commended.*

Shropshire

LONGMYND HOTEL,
Church Stretton,
Shropshire SY6 6AG

Tel: 0694 722244
Fax: 0694 722718

Fully licensed; 50 bedrooms, all with private bathrooms; Historic interest; Children and pets welcome; Car park (100); Ludlow 15 miles, Shrewsbury 13; ££.

Perched high above the pleasant town of Church Stretton in grounds of ten acres, this fine hotel enjoys sweeping views over the beautiful Welsh border country. A subtle mixture of superb modern and period rooms, the hotel possesses outstanding amenities. Luxury suites and bedrooms are equipped with every refinement demanded by the discerning guest of today, backed by activity attractions in the form of an outdoor heated swimming pool (covered in winter months), 9-hole pitch-and-putt course, trim gym and also the tonic of a sauna and solarium. Riding, fishing, shooting and gliding may also be arranged nearby. The cuisine is noteworthy for its excellence and variety and there are superb facilities for conferences and other functions. There are also self-catering lodges in the hotel grounds. 🐾 🐾 🐾 🐾, ***, *Johansens, Ashley Courtenay.*

THE REDFERN HOTEL,
Cleobury Mortimer,
Shropshire DY14 8AA

Tel: 0299 270395

Fax: 0299 271011 Telex: 335176

Licensed; 11 bedrooms, all with private bathrooms or showers; Children and dogs welcome; Car park; Ludlow 11 miles, Bewdley 8; ££/£££.

For centuries past travellers have stayed in the old market town of Cleobury Mortimer. Now a conservation area on the edge of the 6000-acre Forest of Wyre, it forms a perfect centre for exploring the Welsh Marches, Ironbridge Industrial Museum and 2000 years of English history. The shire horses at Acton Scott Farm Museum and the steam engines on the Severn Valley railway will conjure up nostalgia of times past. After a day's adventuring or walking in the Shropshire hills, what better place to relax than in this warm and comfortable hotel, where good fresh food, fine wines and friendly service will make your stay one to remember. All bedrooms have tea/coffee making facilities, baby-listening, hairdryer and direct-dial telephone. Bargain breaks available throughout the year *ETB* 👑 👑 👑 👑, *AA and RAC**.*

OVERTON GRANGE HOTEL,
Ludlow,
Shropshire SY8 4AD

Tel: 0584 87 3500

Licensed; 16 bedrooms, 13 with private bathrooms; Car park (84); London 160 miles, Shrewsbury 29, Worcester 23, Hereford 22; ££.

The beautiful and historic town of Ludlow has many places of interest, not least of which is its impressive 11th century castle overlooking the River Teme. The Edwardian mansion of Overton is a recommended place in which to stay whilst undertaking a leisurely exploration of this delightful part of England. Its guest rooms are extremely well-appointed with unrivalled views over the Shropshire countryside. All have tea and coffee making facilities, colour television, radio and direct-dial telephone. In winter the bar is warmed by log fires, and our oak-panelled restaurant has excellent table d'hôte and à la carte dishes. The Shropshire Hills are of great scenic beauty, and the town also has a steeplechase course and an 18-hole golf course. 👑 👑 👑 👑, *AA and RAC***.*

HUNDRED HOUSE HOTEL,
Bridgnorth Road, Norton, Near Shifnal, Shropshire TF11 9EE

Tel: 095271 353
Fax: 095271 355

Fully licensed; 9 bedrooms, all with private bathrooms; Historic interest; Children welcome; Car park (50); Bridgnorth 4 miles; £££.

This mellow redbrick establishment combines all the qualities most desirable in a first class hostelry. Overnight accommodation offers both comfort and elegance, even the standard rooms having ensuite bathroom, clock and radio alarm, colour television, telephone, tea and coffee tray and ironing facilities. Cuisine is traditionally English, using local produce where possible and herbs from the hotel garden in dishes which will delight the most demanding, whether the choice has been one of the wholesome bar meals served all day, or the more elaborate fare of the intimate à la carte restaurant. *HETB* 🏵 🏵 🏵 🏵 *Highly Commended, RAC Merit Award for Comfort, Hospitality and Restaurant; Les Routiers Casserole Award 1990/1.*

HAWKSTONE PARK HOTEL,
Weston under Redcastle, Shrewsbury, Shropshire SY4 5UY

Tel: 0939 200611
Fax: 0939 200311

Fully licensed; 59 bedrooms, all with private bathrooms; Historic interest; Children welcome, guide dogs only; Car park (300); Wem 3 miles; ££.

With a fine reputation for its accommodation and cuisine, this busy golfing country hotel is set in 400 acres of parkland and antiquities. Sandy Lyle learned his game here and the residential golfing breaks are both popular and reasonably priced. Since the 1920's, the Hawkstone course has challenged the skill of many a famous golfer. Pro-shop facilities for golfers include expert tuition with video analysis. In landscaped grounds of wooded cliffs, valleys and romantic ruins, Hawkstone has many pleasures to offer apart from golf. There are opportunities for antiquity walks, clay pigeon shooting and archery. Tennis and croquet and the outdoor swimming pool are open from May to September. Non-residents are also most warmly welcomed to our very comfortable atmosphere, attended by our friendly staff. 🏵 🏵 🏵 🏵 🏵.

DODINGTON LODGE HOTEL,
Whitchurch, Shropshire SY13 1EN

Tel: 0948 2539

Licensed; 10 bedrooms, all with private bathrooms; Historic interest; Children and pets welcome; Car park (100); Shrewsbury 18 miles; £££.

This supremely comfortable, family-run hotel is a listed building dating from late Georgian times and the expansive ambience of the period remains, keeping happy company with the fine modern amenities that have been introduced. En suite accommodation offers colour television, direct-dial telephone and tea and coffee-making facilities and the restaurant is renowned for its high standard of cuisine. This is a most hospitable venue on the A41 within 20 minutes' drive of Chester and Shrewsbury and its proximity to Telford and the Potteries renders it a popular rendezvous for conferences and social functions. Special golfing weekends in arrangement with Hill Valley, Hawkstone Park and Market Drayton Golf Courses may also be organised to suit personal requirements. 🏵 🏵 🏵 🏵, *AA and RAC ***.*

**If you've found
RECOMMENDED COUNTRY HOTELS
of service please tell your friends**

ROWTON CASTLE HOTEL,
Shrewsbury,
Shropshire SY5 9EP

Tel: 0743 884044

Fax: 0743 884949

Fully licensed; 19 bedrooms, all with private bathrooms; Historic interest; Children and pets welcome; Car park (120); Birmingham 39 miles; ££££.

Although set in the tranquil countryside of one of England's most beautiful counties, imposing and picturesque Rowton Castle is only 10 minutes from the historic market town of Shrewsbury. Standing sedately in 20 acres of grounds which include the largest cedar tree in the country, it has been magically transformed into a hotel of distinction blessed with a superb restaurant, spacious and well-equipped accommodation and extensive banqueting facilities. The history of this somewhat unusual tourist venue is absorbing. Originally mentioned in the Domesday Book and occupying the site of a Roman fort, the castle was destroyed by Llewellyn, Prince of Wales, in 1282 and although part of the large tower is reputed to be from the original building, the main house dates from the turn of the 17th century with additions made two centuries later. The property was made over to Baron Rowton in 1880, a title created as a reward for serving as Disraeli's private secretary. Still retaining many fascinating historic features, the hotel is delightfully furnished and appointed in keeping with its ornate and opulent origins, yet guests will lack nothing in the way of modern refinements. With its magnificent carved oak fireplace, the restaurant presents an extensive à la carte selection and the 18th century Oak Room can seat up to 20 guests in boardroom style for private functions. The splendid, self-contained Cardeston Suite is the perfect venue for conferences and receptions. *HETB* 🌺 🌺 🌺 🌺 🌺 *Highly Commended, Johansens.*

Somerset

SHRUB FARM COUNTRY HOUSE HOTEL,
Burton Row, Brent Knoll,
Somerset TA9 4BX

Tel: 0278 760479

Licensed; All bedrooms with private bathrooms; Historic interest; Children and pets welcome; Car park; Bristol 24 miles, Wells 15; £.

Shrub Farm Country House Hotel is a 500-year-old farmhouse of immense character, set in four acres of beautiful countryside on the edge of the village. This family-run hotel is ideal for a short break, main holiday or overnight stop, being close to Junction 22 of the M5. It is just two miles from the sea, yet close to the Mendip Hills, Sedgemoor and the Quantock Forest, with easy access to Cheddar, Wookey, Wells, Bath, Glastonbury and many other places of interest. All rooms are en suite, with satellite television, direct-dial telephone, tea/coffee facilities, trouser press and hair dryer. The hotel has central heating and a log fire burns on chillier evenings. *ETB* 🐦 🐦 🐦 🐦 *Commended, AA and RAC**.*

CARNARVON ARMS HOTEL,
Dulverton,
Somerset TA22 9AE

Tel: 0398 23302*
Fax: 0398 24022

Licensed; 25 bedrooms, all with private bathrooms; Children and dogs welcome; Car park; Exeter 27 miles, Taunton 26; ££.

Set close to the river in the lovely Barle Valley of the Exmoor National Park, this fine sporting hotel has some five miles of excellent salmon and trout fishing. Standing in its own 50 acres, it has a secluded garden with a heated pool, a hard tennis court, croquet on the lawn, stabling for ten horses, and indoors, a full-sized billiard room. The impressive stone-built Victorian hotel offers the very best of everything, with a fine reputation for its food and wine list, and for a warm and unpretentious atmosphere. Owned and personally run by Mrs Toni Jones for over 34 years, the hotel is a regular haven for many and a happy discovery to others.

BILBROOK LAWNS HOTEL,
Bilbrook, Near Minehead,
Somerset TA24 6HE

Tel: 0984 40331*

Residential and restaurant licence; 7 bedrooms, 4 with private bathrooms; Children and dogs welcome; Car park (8); Dunster 3 miles; £.

With a view of the rolling, wooded Brendon Hills and the rugged splendour of the Exmoor National Park, Bilbrook is an idyllic village in an area often bypassed by holidaymakers. In such a delightful setting lies Bilbrook Lawns, a lovely country house offering comfortable accommodation, tranquillity and friendly service to say nothing of superb food and wines under the personal supervision of Resident Proprietors, Roy and Barbara Whymark. All the bedrooms are on the first floor and incorporate television and tea and coffee-making facilities. Bilbrook has an interesting ford, a fascination for children, and nearby is the picture-book village of Old Cleeve with its thatched houses whilst Dunster Castle and the resort of Minehead are just two of the nearby places of interest. 🐦 🐦 🐦 *Approved, AA*, RAC Acclaimed.*

BATCH FARM COUNTRY HOTEL,
Lympsham, Near Weston-super-Mare,
Somerset BS24 0EX

Tel: 0934 750371*

Restaurant and residential licence; 8 bedrooms, all with private bathrooms; Historic interest; Children welcome; Car park (50); Weston-super-Mare 5 miles, Burnham-on-Sea 4; £/££.

An air of old world charm pervades Batch Farm Country Hotel, lending atmosphere to the modern accommodation. Guests are welcome here all year except Christmas, and the eight bedrooms (all en suite) are comfortably fitted and have colour television and tea/coffee facilities. All enjoy panoramic views of hills and countryside. For guests' relaxation there is a fully licensed lounge bar and three lounges, one with colour television. Traditional home cooking using local produce and home reared beef when possible is offered in the à la carte restaurant. Fishing is available in the grounds, and riding, swimming, tennis and golf are to be found locally. Ample parking in own grounds. Batch Farm Country Hotel is ideal for touring, being three miles from sea and sands, and midway between Weston and Burnham-on-Sea, with Cheddar, Wells, Longleat, Bristol and Bath all within easy reach. Personal attention from the resident proprietors will ensure that your holiday is a happy one. Most credit cards accepted. Brochure. *AA and RAC**; Egon Ronay; Ashley Courtenay Recommended.*

RALEIGH MANOR,
Wheddon Cross,
Somerset TA24 7BB

Tel: 0643 841484*

Residential licence; 7 bedrooms, all with private bathrooms; Car park (10); Exeter 37 miles, Minehead 9; ££.

Raleigh Manor is an elegant nineteenth-century Manor House standing within Exmoor National Park. From wooded grounds of over an acre the hotel enjoys superb views across Exmoor, Snowdrop Valley and the Bristol Channel. A bridle path leads from the hotel grounds to Dunkery Beacon. The hotel is furnished with antiques and has two comfortable lounges with log fires. All seven bedrooms are en suite, and have tea/coffee making facilities and colour television. The Squire's Bedroom features a magnificent half-tester bed. The hotel restaurant serves traditional home-cooked fare and a selection of quality wines. *AA**.*

WESTERCLOSE COUNTRY HOUSE HOTEL,
Withypool,
Somerset TA24 7QR

Tel: 064-383 302

Licensed; 10 bedrooms, all with private bathrooms; Children welcome; Car park (14); Exford 2 miles; £.

Our country house hotel nestles in the heart of Exmoor, set in nine acres of its own land, complete with donkeys and chickens! Bedrooms are all en suite and charmingly furnished. Our guests can relax in the conservatory bar in summer or settle in front of a log fire in comfortable chairs in winter. Endless walks and places of interest to visit will leave you spoilt for choice and ready to enjoy a meal in our excellent restaurant, which specialises in English West Country and vegetarian dishes, accompanied by any of the wines from our hand-picked (and tasted!) list. ☙ ☙ ☙ *Commended, AA and RAC**.*

GLENCOT HOUSE,
Glencot Lane, Wookey Hole,
Near Wells, Somerset BA5 1BH

Tel: 0749 677160
Fax: 0749 670210

Restaurant and residential licence; 12 bedrooms, all with private bathrooms; Historic interest; Children and well-behaved pets welcome; Car park (20); Wells 2 miles; ££.

Set in 18 acres of garden and parkland with river frontage, this elegantly furnished Victorian mansion offers high class accommodation, excellent cuisine with friendly service, and homely atmosphere. All the rooms are individually decorated and furnished, enjoy lovely views, have en suite facilities, tea and coffee, colour television, direct-dial telephone and central heating. There is also a sauna, solarium, small indoor jet-stream pool, snooker, table tennis and private fishing. Glencot is ideally situated for the tourist who wishes to explore the beautiful Mendip Hills and many places of interest in Somerset. The hotel also caters for conferences and small private functions. Children and pets are welcome. Open all year.

SOMERSET – THE CREAM AND CIDER COUNTY!

Wookey Hole, the great cave near Wells, is the first known home of man in Great Britain. Other places of interest in this green and hilly county include The Mendips, Exmoor National Park, Cheddar Gorge, Meare Lake Village and The Somerset Rural Life Museum. The villages and wildlife of the Quantocks, Poldens and Brendons should not be missed.

Staffordshire

THE BROOKHOUSE HOTEL,
Brookside, Rolleston-on-Dove,
Burton-on-Trent, Staffordshire DE13 9AA

Tel: 0283 814188
Fax: 0283 813644

Licensed; 19 bedrooms, all with private bathrooms; Historic interest; Children over 12 years welcome; Car park (70); Burton-on-Trent 4 miles; £££/££££.

Beautifully furnished with antiques and some original works of art, this is a William and Mary Grade II Listed building of special architectural and historic interest, which was skilfully converted into a hotel of some style in 1976. Dining here is an experience to be savoured, imaginative dishes being presented in the company of crystal and silver, fresh flowers and candlelight. Food is freshly cooked to order and there is a comprehensive list of wines, some rare and unusual. Bedrooms are individually planned with antique furniture, and many have four-poster, half-tester or Victorian brass beds, trimmed with Nottingham lace. Four ground floor bedrooms are suitable for partially disabled guests. Good facilities exist for conferences and other functions. 🐾 🐾 🐾 🐾 *Commended, Egon Ronay, Ashley Courtenay.*

YE OLDE DOG AND PARTRIDGE HOTEL,
High Street, Tutbury, Burton-upon-Trent,
Staffordshire DE13 9LS

Tel: 0283 813030
Fax: 0283 813178

Fully licensed; 17 bedrooms, all with private bathrooms; Historic interest; Children and pets welcome; Car park (80); Derby 11 miles, Burton-upon-Trent 4; £££.

One of the most enchanting buildings in Tutbury's High Street, with flower-filled baskets and window boxes decorating its splendid oak-beamed frontage, this 500-year-old coaching inn tempts all to cross its threshold and loiter awhile. Two bars offer a choice of venue to partake of refreshment, and those seeking sustenance have the formal surroundings of the Carvery Rotisserie, where live music on the grand piano provides a background for the extensive display of wholesome hot and cold fare. Bedrooms, reached by an elegant Georgian spiral staircase, have television, fridge bar, tea and coffee facilities, hairdryer, radio alarm and luxury bathroom en suite. Some four-poster rooms are available. 🐾 🐾 🐾 🐾, *AA***, RAC*** Merit Award, BTA Commended, Egon Ronay.*

Suffolk

PRIORY HOTEL,
Tollgate, Bury St. Edmunds,
Suffolk IP32 6EH

Tel: 0284 766181
Fax: 0284 767604

Hotel and restaurant licence; 27 bedrooms, all with private bathrooms; Historic interest; Children welcome, pets by arrangement; Car park (70); Ely 24 miles, Newmarket 14; £££.

The history books say The Priory was founded in 1263 with rebuilding on the site carried out in the 16th century. Since then, many alterations and extensions have been carried out but something of the former ambience remains to fascinate the modern-day visitor to this quiet and attractive town. Although its foundations are set firmly in the past, The Priory is now equipped with every modern facility to ensure a memorable sojourn and the à la carte cuisine, featuring traditional English and French dishes, has an enviable reputation. Full of character and charmingly furnished, guest rooms are blessed with private bathroom and shower, remote-control colour television, direct-dial telephone and tea and coffee-makers. Conference and function facilities are amongst the very best in the area. 👑 👑 👑 👑 *Highly Commended; AA*** and Rosette.*

BROME GRANGE HOTEL,
Brome, Eye,
Suffolk IP23 8AP

Tel: 0379 8704
Fax: 0379 870921

Fully licensed; 22 bedrooms, all with private bathrooms; Historic interest; Children and pets welcome; Norwich 20 miles, Bury St Edmunds 20; ££.

A characterful sixteenth-century hotel with 22 chalet-style bedrooms set in mature grounds. Excellent food is served in the restaurant under the personal supervision of the chef patron. Guests enjoy most friendly and attentive service. 👑 👑 👑 👑 *Commended.*

MILL HOTEL,
Walnut Tree Lane, Sudbury,
Suffolk CO10 6BD

Tel: 0787 75544
Fax: 0787 73027

Fully licensed; 50 bedrooms, all with private bathrooms; Historic interest; Children and pets welcome; Car park (60); Ipswich 21 miles, Colchester 14; £££.

The artist, Thomas Gainsborough, was born in Sudbury and his former house is now a museum and art gallery; John Constable made familiar the tranquil Suffolk scene through his idyllic landscapes and it might be trite to say that the manner in which the Mill Hotel serves as a holiday and business centre is an art form in itself. Surrounded by water meadows, the bar overlooks the mill pool and the restaurant is actually situated in the old millhouse. Quiet guest rooms are attractively appointed; all are centrally heated and have bathrooms en suite, colour television, radio, telephone and tea and coffee-making facilities. The hotel holds fishing rights on an adjacent stretch of the River Stour and golf is available two miles away. 👙 👙 👙 👙, ***.

Key to
Tourist Board Ratings

The Crown Scheme
(England, Scotland & Wales)

Covering hotels, motels, private hotels, guesthouses, inns, bed & breakfast, farmhouses. Every Crown classified place to stay is inspected annually. *The classification:* Listed then 1-5 Crown indicates the range of facilities and services. Higher quality standards are indicated by the terms APPROVED, COMMENDED, HIGHLY COMMENDED and DELUXE.

The Key Scheme
(also operates in Scotland using a Crown symbol)

Covering self-catering in cottages, bungalows, flats, houseboats, houses, chalets, etc. Every Key classified holiday home is inspected annually. *The classification:* 1-5 Key indicates the range of facilities and equipment. Higher quality standards are indicated by the terms APPROVED, COMMENDED, HIGHLY COMMENDED and DELUXE.

The Q Scheme
(England, Scotland & Wales)

Covering holiday, caravan, chalet and camping parks. Every Q rated park is inspected annually for its quality standards. The more √ in the Q – up to 5 – the higher the standard of what is provided.

Surrey

BOOKHAM GRANGE HOTEL,
Little Bookham Common, Bookham, Leatherhead,
Surrey KT23 3HS
Tel: 0372 452742; Fax: 0372 450080

Fully licensed; 17 bedrooms, all with private bathrooms; Children welcome, pets by arrangement; Car park (150); Leatherhead 2 miles; ££££.

The landscaped gardens of this charming old English country house form a picturesque setting. In an area abounding in pleasant country walks and actually on the edge of the delightful Bookham Common, the hotel is also conveniently placed for excursions to London (45 minutes by train from the nearby station). Splendidly furnished and appointed throughout, Bookham Grange is the ideal place for combining urban and rural pursuits and there are many places of interest in the vicinity as well as excellent theatres at Leatherhead and Guildford. The Polesden Room Restaurant is well regarded for its exciting selection of English and international dishes. The facilities available for special social functions and conferences are superb. ♚ ♚ ♚ ♚.

The **£** symbol when appearing at the end of the italic section of an entry shows the anticipated price, during 1993, for a **single room with English Breakfast.**

Under £30	**£**	**Over £45 but under £60**	**£££**
Over £30 but under £45	**££**	**Over £60**	**££££**

This is meant as an indication only and does not show prices for Special Breaks, Weekends, etc. Guests are therefore advised to verify all prices on enquiring or booking.

GATTON MANOR HOTEL, GOLF & COUNTRY CLUB,
Ockley, Near Dorking,
Surrey RH5 5PQ

Tel: 0306-79 555

Fax: 0306-79 713

Fully licensed; 10 bedrooms, all with private bathrooms; Children welcome; Horsham 6 miles; £££.

A perfect holiday complex and conference venue within easy reach of London and the quiet Surrey countryside, this 18th century manor house not only has magnificently appointed accommodation but a superb 18-hole golf course of its own in addition to a driving range and putting green. Set in 200 acres of gardens and parkland teeming with a variety of wildlife and approached via a long drive of oak trees, this imposing place also has three well-stocked lakes offering excellent coarse and trout fishing, and a bowling green. Twin and double bedrooms all have en suite facilities and the à la carte cuisine is highly regarded. The hotel is well versed in buffet and function arrangements and two fine conference rooms seat 60 and 30 people. *SETB* ♛ ♛ ♛.

East Sussex

WINSTON MANOR HOTEL,
Beacon Road, Crowborough,
East Sussex TN6 1AD

Tel: 0892 652772

Fax: 0892 665537

Fully licensed; 50 bedrooms, all with private bathrooms; Children welcome; Car park (70); London 44 miles; ££.

Proud of its standards of Sussex hospitality, this privately-owned hotel is located in the pleasant town of Crowborough, high in the heart of the Ashdown Forest. With beautiful scenery close at hand and with the coast within easy motoring distance, this superbly appointed establishment is of great appeal to touring holidaymakers. Nevertheless, businessmen also find this conveniently placed retreat an ideal port of call for the conference and function arrangements are magnificent. With spacious public and private rooms, the hotel is tastefully decorated throughout. Guest rooms all have en suite amenities and choosing from full à la carte and table d'hôte menus available in a delightful restaurant is a pleasure in itself. Leisure facilities include a swimming pool with jetstream, jacuzzi, sauna and fully-equipped gymnasium, and are complemented by an all-day coffee shop offering teas, coffees, snacks and light meals.

BEAUPORT PARK HOTEL,
Battle Road, Hastings,
East Sussex TN38 8EA

Tel: 0424 851222
Fax: 0424 852465

Licensed; 16 double bedrooms, 7 single, all with bathrooms; Car park; Battle 3 miles, Hastings 3; ££.

This fine three-star country house hotel, set amidst 33 acres of woodland and picturesque formal gardens, offers old-fashioned personal service from resident directors Kenneth and Helena Melsom. All guest rooms have private bathrooms and are equipped with remote-control colour television, electric trouser press, direct-dial telephone, hairdryer and tea/coffee making facilities. There is a heated swimming pool in the grounds, country walks, tennis courts, croquet lawn, badminton, outdoor chess, French boules, and putting green, with an 18-hole golf course, riding stables and squash courts adjoining. Prospective guests are invited to write or telephone for brochure and tariff, and a country house bargain breaks leaflet. "Country House Getaway Breaks" are available all year. 🐦🐦🐦🐦.

CLEAVERS LYNG COUNTRY HOTEL,
Church Road, Herstmonceux,
East Sussex BN27 1QJ

Tel: 0323 833131
Fax: 0323 833617

Fully licensed; 8 bedrooms; Historic interest; Children and pets welcome; Car park (15); Eastbourne 11 miles; £.

For good home cooking in traditional English style, comfort and informality, this little family-run hotel in the heart of rural East Sussex is well recommended. Peacefully set in lovely gardens, adjacent to Herstmonceux Castle, the house dates from 1580 as its oak beams and inglenook fireplace bear witness. No glitter or glitz, this is an ideal retreat for a quiet sojourn away from urban clamour. The castles at Pevensey, Scotney, Bodiam and Hever are all within easy reach as are Battle Abbey, Kipling's house, Batemans, Michelham Priory and the seaside resorts of Eastbourne and Hastings. Bedrooms all have central heating, wash-hand basins and tea-making facilities and there is a small bar and television lounge.

BOSHIP FARM HOTEL,
Lower Dicker, Near Hailsham,
East Sussex BN27 4AT

Tel: 0323 844826
Fax: 0323 843945

Fully licensed; 46 bedrooms, all with private bathrooms; Historic interest; Children and dogs welcome; Car park (200); Hailsham 3 miles; ££.

Only 36 miles from Gatwick Airport, within easy reach of the south coast and surrounded by open country, this well recommended hotel is a fascinating place in which to stay. A lovely old farmhouse, dating from 1652, forms the main part of the hotel, still furnished with original beams and timbers and a magnificent brick fireplace with genuine Charles II wrought-iron backplate. Beautifully appointed bedrooms are individually decorated to a high standard, all with private bathroom, colour television, radio, direct-dial telephone, hair-dryer, trouser press and tea and coffee-making facilities. Next to a comfortable lounge is the elegant restaurant renowned for its excellent cuisine. Amenities include an indoor health suite and a tennis court and a fine swimming pool in the grounds. 🐦🐦🐦🐦, *RAC ****.

LITTLE ORCHARD HOUSE,
West Street, Rye,
East Sussex TN31 7ES

Tel: 0797 223831

3 bedrooms, all with private bathrooms; Historic interest; London 67 miles, Canterbury 33, Battle 14, Tenterden 12; £/££.

Rye is the most complete small medieval hill town in Britain, and this charming Georgian townhouse is a delightful surprise right at the heart of the Ancient Town, quietly situated in the picturesque cobbled streets with a traditional walled Old English garden and its unique Smugglers Watch Tower. Each bedroom, one with traditional four-poster, has a bathroom en suite, colour TV and hot drinks making facilities. The house is stylishly decorated and furnished with antiques throughout, lots of books, paintings, and an open fire in winter. Guests will enjoy a generous country breakfast which features as much local, organic produce as possible, and a good choice of outstanding restaurants are within easy walking distance.

DALE HILL GOLF HOTEL,
Ticehurst, Wadhurst,
East Sussex TN5 7DQ

Tel: 0580 200112

Licensed; 26 bedrooms, all with private bathrooms; Car park; Wadhurst 3 miles; ££££.

The warmest of welcomes awaits you at one of England's finest new hotels. Set in 300 acres of beautiful grounds, its en suite bedrooms with excellent room service facilities make Dale Hill a delightful experience. A small luxury leisure centre with indoor swimming pool and full beauty and massage treatments, together with a superb 18-hole established parkland golf course and award-winning restaurant all add up to the luxury you deserve. *ETB* 🌷 🌷 🌷 🌷 🌷 *Highly Commended, AA and RAC**** and Restaurant Rosette.* **See also Colour Advertisement p.11.**

THE COUNTRY HOUSE AT WINCHELSEA,
Hastings Road, Winchelsea,
East Sussex TN36 4AD

Tel: 0797 226669

Restaurant licence; 3 bedrooms, all with en suite or private facilities; Children over 9 years welcome; Car parking; London 75 miles, Dover 39, Rye 3; £.

A delightful setting and wonderful country views make our 17th century Listed home an ideal choice for that "Special Break". Comfortable, pretty bedrooms with en suite or private facilities, colour television, direct-dial telephone and complimentary hot drinks tray. There is a cosy sitting room with log fire for those chillier evenings, and you may also enjoy a pre-dinner aperitif in the lounge bar. In the elegant candlelit dining room only the finest local produce is served with friendliness and care. Ample parking in the grounds. Please write or telephone Mary Carmichael for a brochure and tariff. *ETB* 🌷 🌷 🌷 🌷 *Highly Commended, AA Selected House.*

West Sussex

MILLSTREAM HOTEL AND RESTAURANT,
Bosham, Chichester,
West Sussex PO18 8HL

Tel: 0243 573234
Fax: 0243 573459

Residential licence; 29 bedrooms, all with private bathrooms; Historic interest; Children and pets welcome; Car park (40); London 64 miles, Chichester 3½; £££.

Idyllically situated in a picturesque sailing village on the shores of Chichester Harbour, this homely country house possesses all the credentials for a relaxing holiday in an atmosphere reminiscent of a more leisurely age. For all that, the amenities here lack nothing in terms of modern sophistication and they blend with subtle deference to period style furnishings. Each of the well-appointed guest rooms is individually decorated and public rooms include a sumptuous drawing room with grand piano, a separate study/sitting room, ideal for games or private parties and also the delightful Malthouse Bar which leads on to a pretty garden complete with its own stream. Dining by candlelight in the restaurant prompts fond memories of exciting and beautifully prepared dishes, exotic sweets and fine vintage wines. 🌷 🌷 🌷 🌷 *Highly Commended, AA** and One Rosette.*

PARK HOUSE HOTEL,
Bepton, Midhurst,
West Sussex GU29 0JB

Tel: 0730 812880
Fax: 0730 815643

Residential licence; 11 bedrooms, all with private bathrooms; Children and pets welcome; Car park (25); Midhurst 3 miles; £££.

A lovely country house in the verdant tranquillity of West Sussex, the fully licensed Park House is happily placed only six miles from Goodwood and within easy reach of Cowdray Park (for polo), the Chichester Festival Theatre, several first-class golf courses and the coast. Delightfully furnished throughout, the house stands in spacious grounds in which are two grass tennis courts, putting and croquet lawns, a 9-hole pitch-and-putt course, and a heated swimming pool. Under the benign care of Resident Proprietor, Mrs I. O'Brien, guest rooms are excellently appointed with bathrooms en suite, colour television and radio telephones. Immediately adjoining the house is a fully serviced cottage annexe with a sitting room, double bedroom, dining room and bathroom. 🌷 🌷 🌷 🌷, *AA ****.*

CHEQUERS HOTEL,
Pulborough,
West Sussex RH20 1AD

Tel: 0798 872486
Fax: 0798 872715

Residential and restaurant licence; 11 bedrooms, all with private bathrooms; Historic interest; Children and dogs welcome; Car park (14); London 49 miles, Brighton 19, Arundel 9; DB&B ££.

Tastefully extended over the years, the original Queen Anne house huddles on the edge of Pulborough village, gazing peacefully out over the Arun Valley to the South Downs beyond. Excellent home-cooked dishes using local produce and fresh vegetables have given Chequers its reputation for fine cuisine. Accommodation is comfortable and well appointed with private bathrooms, and also includes colour TV, direct-dial telephone, trouser press, hairdryer and tea/coffee facilities. Four-poster bedrooms and ground floor bedrooms also available. Open fires make this as pleasant a holiday venue in winter as it is in summer. Places to visit include Parham, Petworth, Goodwood, Arundel, Chichester and the Weald & Downland Open Air Museum. New garden conservatory. Bargain breaks are available throughout the year. *ETB* 🏵🏵🏵🏵, *RAC and AA**, Ashley Courtenay and Egon Ronay Recommended.*

Warwickshire

CROWN & CUSHION HOTEL AND LEISURE CENTRE,
Chipping Norton,
Freephone for brochure: 0800 585251
Near Stratford-upon-Avon OX7 5AD
Fax: 0608 642926

Fully licensed; 40 bedrooms, all with private bathrooms; Historic interest; Children and pets welcome; Car park (30); Stratford-upon-Avon 21 miles; ££.

Five-hundred-year-old coaching inn, tastefully modernised to provide 40 excellent en suite bedrooms; some four-poster suites. Among its many attractions are an "old world" bar, log fires, real ale and good food. Facilities include an indoor pool, squash court, multi-gym, solarium; full size snooker table subject to availability. There is also a fully equipped modern conference centre. The hotel is located in a picturesque Cotswolds town midway between Oxford and Stratford-upon-Avon, convenient for London, Heathrow Airport and M40 motorway. Blenheim Palace, Warwick Castle, Broadway, Bourton-on-the-Water, Bibury, Stow-on-the-Wold and Shakespeare Country are all nearby. *ETB* 🌸 🌸 🌸 🌸 *Approved, Egon Ronay, Ashley Courtenay, Les Routiers.*

EATHORPE PARK HOTEL,
Fosse Way, Eathorpe, Leamington Spa,
Warwickshire CV33 9DQ
Tel: 0926 632632

Fully licensed; 18 bedrooms, all with private bathrooms; Historic interest; Children welcome; Car park (200); Leamington Spa 6 miles, Southam 5; £££.

A Victorian house with eighteen en suite bedrooms, set amidst eleven acres of parkland, with breathtaking views and a friendly, family atmosphere. Ideally situated for visiting many places of historic interest such as Warwick, Coventry, Stratford-upon-Avon and Leamington Spa. Four major motorways, the National Exhibition Centre and National Agricultural Centre are close by. Our à la carte restaurant will provide you with a rich experience. The bar meal menu is extensive and varied, and competes with the restaurant. Special weekend breaks available. *AA**.*

West Midlands

BROOKLANDS GRANGE HOTEL,
Holyhead Road, Coventry,
West Midlands CV5 8HX

Tel: 0203 601601

Fax: 0203 601277

Fully licensed; 30 bedrooms, all with private bathrooms; Historic interest; Children welcome; Car park (54); Birmingham 17 miles; ££££.

Peacefully reposing in spacious grounds, this tastefully restored Jacobean farmhouse is, somewhat surprisingly, only 2 miles from the city centre. As such, it is conveniently placed for a multitude of cultural and sporting attractions and there are pleasant walks to be had in the immediate vicinity. By virtue of its position and specialised amenities, the hotel is a popular venue for conferences and social functions. The Bridal Suite is a splendid and spacious Victorian room and is delightfully furnished. Oak beams and low ceilings contribute to the character of this charming hotel. Dating from the 16th century and enlarged during Victorian times, further new bedrooms have since been added to give variety of choice. Ancient or modern, they all have a common theme — attractive decor, supreme comfort and up-to-date appointments that include bathrooms en suite, direct-dial telephone, television, radio, in-house video, trouser press and hair dryer. With its imaginative and selective menu, the elegant restaurant offers the best in contemporary English cooking, excellent dishes enhanced perhaps by a prior visit to the 16th century cocktail bar. Recommended on many counts, this is a prestigious, privately-owned hotel where a courteous and efficient staff makes every effort to ensure the well-being of guests. ♛ ♛ ♛ ♛ *Commended, AA and RAC ***.*

NOTE

All the information in this book is given in good faith in the belief that it is correct. However, the publishers cannot guarantee the facts given in these pages, neither are they responsible for changes in policy, ownership or terms that may take place after the date of going to press. Readers should always satisfy themselves that the facilities they require are available and that the terms, if quoted, still apply.

Wiltshire

BLUNSDON HOUSE HOTEL,
Blunsdon, Swindon,
Wiltshire SN2 4AD

Tel: 0793 721701
Fax: 0793 721056

Fully licensed; 88 bedrooms, all with private bathrooms; Children welcome; Car park (300); Swindon 4 miles; ££££.

Blossoming from humble beginnings as a farm guest house in 1957 to the superb 4-star hotel it is today has been a remarkable transfiguration, for the hotel and leisure facilities available here are surely amongst the very best in the country. Decorated and furnished to the highest possible standards, guest rooms lack nothing in their provision of sophisticated and practical appointments. The reasonable tariff includes a full English breakfast and use of swimming and spa pools, squash, gymnasium, tennis court, jogging track, sauna and steam rooms in the fabulous Leisure Club. One may dine splendidly in style in the attractive Ridge Restaurant or, more informally, in Carrie's Carverie, known for its prime roast joints and range of entrée dishes. Children are exceptionally well cared for at this enlightened venue. The use of a supervised crèche is provided free at specified times and baby listening and sitting may easily be arranged. There is also a large playroom with computer games and a toddlers' splash pool. Spacious, light and airy, this fine, family-run hotel is an ideal place for active or passive relaxation; just strolling through the wooded grounds is a pleasure in itself. Little wonder, therefore, that the purpose-designed conference and function rooms are put to such good use. There is free parking for 300 vehicles and a helipad for high flyers. 🌟 🌟 🌟 🌟 🌟, *UK Hotel of the Year 1990, AA Courtesy and Care Award Winner 1991, RAC Merit Award.*

Worcestershire

NIGHTINGALE,
Bishampton, Pershore,
Worcestershire WR10 2NH

Tel: 038-682 521

Licensed; 4 bedrooms, all with private bathrooms; Children and pets welcome; Stratford-upon-Avon 16 miles, Pershore 5; ££.

This small hotel in the Vale of Evesham in the Heart of England lies close to the Cotswolds, Stratford-upon-Avon, Malvern and Worcester. There is an international golf course (9 holes and 18 holes) just five minutes from here, riding stables just a few miles away, and plenty of sports amenities. The excellent home cooking in the restaurant is well-known for miles around, specialising in Shetland smoked salmon, certified Aberdeen Angus beef and home-made ice creams. Sorry no dogs. ♣ ♣ ♣ *Highly Commended, AA Selected QQQQ.*

EVESHAM HOTEL,
Coopers Lane (off Waterside), Evesham,
Worcestershire WR11 6DA

Tel: 0386 765566
Fax: 0386 765443

Fully licensed; 40 bedrooms, all with private bathrooms; Historic interest; Children and pets welcome; Car park (50); Worcester 16 miles, Stratford-upon-Avon 14; ££££.

Enthusiastically run by the Jenkinson family, aided by a happy and efficient staff, this warmly welcoming Georgian manor house has a long history that goes back to 1540 although it was 'modernised' in Georgian style in 1810. Standing in 2½ acres of grounds within strolling distance of the town centre, the hotel boasts individually decorated guest rooms appointed in contemporary style with bathrooms en suite, colour television, radio, telephone and, for the young in years or heart, even a rubber duck and teddy! Food is subject to general approbation whether it be the traditional English breakfast, lunchtime buffet or a superb dinner served in the attractive Cedars Restaurant, dishes being complemented by a remarkable selection of wines. ♣ ♣ ♣ ♣ *Commended, ***.*

THE MILL AT HARVINGTON,
Anchor Lane, Harvington, Evesham,
Worcestershire WR11 5NR
Tel: 0386 870688*

Restaurant and residential licence; 15 bedrooms, all with private bathrooms; Historic interest; Children over 10 years welcome; Car park (40); Evesham 3 miles; £££.

Beautifully placed on the banks of the peaceful Avon as it winds its way from Stratford to the Severn, the enchanting Mill at Harvington has served the community in a variety of guises since it was built in 1750. It has been, in turn, a malting mill, brewery and bread mill before embarking on its present distinctive career as a first-class country hotel. Sensitively modernised, the hotel stands in almost 8 acres of wooded parkland with 600 ft. of river frontage from which guests may enjoy excellent fishing and boating. Other sporting attractions in the grounds include a hard tennis court and heated swimming pool; and, in addition for nature lovers, there is a fascinating variety of wildlife to be viewed. Guest rooms are bright and cheerful and delightfully appointed with bathrooms en suite, colour television, radio, telephone and tea and coffee-making facilities. Special provision has been made for wheelchair access in certain bedrooms and bathrooms. With views across the garden, the elegant decorated restaurant is an attractive setting for contemplation and enjoyment of dishes from an interesting and frequently changed menu, much use being made of local produce. The restaurant, which seats 30, is also a fine venue for a variety of social functions. If one can tear oneself away from this idyllic retreat, there are numerous places of historic interest within easy reach to say nothing of Shakespeare's England, Stratford being only 10 miles away. 🏵 🏵 🏵 🏵 *Highly Commended; RAC Merit Award, AA Care and Courtesy Awards.*

GAINSBOROUGH HOUSE HOTEL,
Bewdley Hill, Kidderminster,
Worcestershire DY11 6BS
Tel: 0562 820041
Fax: 0562 66179

Fully licensed; 42 bedrooms, all with private bathrooms; Historic interest; Children and pets welcome; Car park (130); Kidderminster 3 miles; £££.

In verdant surroundings on the fringe of the ancient Forest of Wyre, this attractive hotel, a Georgian listed building, is somewhat surprisingly within walking distance of Kidderminster town centre. Exuding the graceful charm of former days, the hotel has been sensitively refurbished and extended over recent years and has built quite a reputation for its hospitality, modern amenities and high standards of traditional service. Guest rooms are appointed to a notable level of comfort; all have bath and shower en suite, television, radio, direct-dial telephone and tea and coffee trays as standard, and non-smoking, executive, family rooms and a four-poster bridal suite are also available. Dining in the Blue Boy Restaurant is a joyful experience, the table d'hôte and à la carte menus presenting a tempting choice of English and Continental dishes backed by a carefully chosen wine list. The hotel is particularly well endowed with facilities for conferences and special functions whether it be a board meeting for 10 or a product launch or banquet for 200. A wide range of audio visual equipment may be supplied. Conveniently placed for so many fascinating places to visit, this fine hotel fully deserves recommendation on all counts and it should be noted that the M5 and national motorway network is just 20 minutes' drive away. 🏵 🏵 🏵 🏵, *RAC Awards for Hospitality and Service.*

North Yorkshire

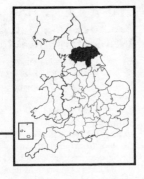

THE SHIP INN,
Acaster Malbis, York,
North Yorkshire YO2 1XB

Tel: 0904 705609/703888
Fax: 0532 429693

Licensed; 8 bedrooms, all with private bathrooms; Historic interest; Children welcome; Car park (50); Leeds 17 miles, York 4; ££.

This friendly and attractive hostelry on the banks of the Ouse is only a short distance from the magnificence of York, the United Kingdom's second most popular tourist attraction. Offering first-class fare and spruce accommodation which includes a four-poster bedroom and a family room, the inn makes a superb holiday headquarters and is equally popular with boating enthusiasts and businessmen. Excellent evening dinners are served in the relaxed olde worlde atmosphere of the restaurant, whilst a wide range of lunches and evening snacks may be enjoyed in the friendly Riverside Bar. Those with a penchant for fishing may be well accommodated, and the inn has its own moorings. Further afield, the Yorkshire Dales beckon, and the coast may be reached in less than an hour. *Tourist Board Listed "Commended", AA Listed.*

THE PARSONAGE COUNTRY HOUSE HOTEL,
Main Street, Escrick, York,
North Yorkshire YO4 6NX

Tel: 0904 728111
Fax: 0904 728151

Fully licensed; 13 bedrooms, all with private bathrooms; Historic interest; Children welcome; Car park (100); York 4 miles; ££££.

The Parsonage Country House Hotel is set back from the road in mature grounds approximately four miles from historic York in the ancient village of Escrick. The hotel, which is an early nineteenth-century former parsonage, reflects an exquisite heritage. Try our intimate dining room and sample wines from our excellent list. German and French spoken. Special rates for two-day short breaks — details on request. 🏵 🏵 🏵 🏵 *Highly Commended, AA***.*

INN ON THE MOOR,
Goathland,
North Yorkshire YO22 5LZ

Tel: 0947 86296
Fax: 0947 86484

Fully licensed; 24 bedrooms, all with private bathrooms; Children welcome, dogs by arrangement; Car park (40); Whitby 7 miles; ££.

Indeed, an imposing country house hotel rather than the popular concept of an inn, this splendidly appointed retreat lies in the pleasant village of Goathland (recently featured in the successful TV series "Heartbeat") in the very heart of the North York Moors National Park; all around a colourful and ever-changing panorama, peace and solitude. The perfect escape from the rigours of a noisy and material world, the hotel is delightfully furnished, a notable feature being the solid oak furniture made by a local craftsman. Spick and span and impeccably clean, these requisites for a memorable holiday are complemented by the superb English cuisine prepared by a highly experienced kitchen and an equally high standard of care and service. 🏵 🏵 🏵 🏵 *Commended, RAC ***.*

WHITFIELD HOUSE HOTEL,
Darnholm, Goathland,
North Yorkshire YO22 5LA

Tel: 0947 86215*

Restaurant and residential licence; 9 bedrooms, all with private bathrooms; Children over 3 welcome, dogs by arrangement; Car park (10); Whitby 9 miles; £.

On the fringe of Goathland in the beautiful North York Moors, we are ideally situated for walking or touring the National Park. The North York Moors Railway is close by, and Whitby and the coast just nine miles away. A former seventeenth-century farmhouse, Whitfield House Hotel offers a warm and friendly atmosphere with personal attention and superb country cuisine. We have nine attractive cottage-style bedrooms, all with en suite bathroom, hairdryer, teamaker, radio and telephone. Central heating throughout. Bar lounge and television lounge. Open from February to November. ♛ ♛ ♛ *Commended.*

FOR THE MUTUAL GUIDANCE
OF GUEST AND HOST

Every year literally thousands of holidays, short-breaks and overnight stops are arranged through our guides, the vast majority without any problems at all. In a handful of cases, however, difficulties do arise about bookings, which often could have been prevented from the outset.

It is important to remember that when accommodation has been booked, both parties — guests and hosts — have entered into a form of contract. We hope that the following points will provide helpful guidance.

GUESTS: When enquiring about accommodation, be as precise as possible. Give exact dates, numbers in your party and the ages of any children. State the number and type of rooms wanted and also what catering you require — bed and breakfast, full board, etc. Make sure that the position about evening meals is clear — and about pets, reductions for children or any other special points.

Read our reviews carefully to ensure that the proprietors you are going to contact can supply what you want. Ask for a letter confirming all arrangements, if possible.

If you have to cancel, do so as soon as possible. Proprietors do have the right to retain deposits and under certain circumstances to charge for cancelled holidays if adequate notice is not given and they cannot re-let the accommodation.

HOSTS: Give details about your facilities and about any special conditions. Explain your deposit system clearly and arrangements for cancellations, charges, etc, and whether or not your terms include VAT.

If for any reason you are unable to fulfil an agreed booking without adequate notice, you may be under an obligation to arrange alternative suitable accommodation or to make some form of compensation.

While every effort is made to ensure accuracy, we regret that FHG Publications cannot accept responsibility for errors, omissions or misrepresentation in our entries or any consequences thereof. Prices in particular should be checked because we go to press early. We will follow up complaints but cannot act as arbiters or agents for either party.

OLD SWAN HOTEL,
Swan Road, Harrogate,
North Yorkshire HG1 2SR

Tel: 0423 500055
Fax: 0423 501154

Fully licensed; 135 bedrooms, all with private bathrooms; Historic interest; Children and pets welcome; Car park (200); York 22 miles, Leeds 15; ££££.

Retaining the elegant air of bygone days to which luxurious appointments have been so skilfully added, the imposing, ivy-clad Old Swan Hotel stands in peaceful gardens yet is only a stone's throw from the heart of perhaps England's most charming inland resort. Every one of the stylish bedrooms and suites has its own bathroom, colour television with free in-house films, direct-dial telephone and hospitality tray whilst facilities for conferences and private functions are first-class. Renowned for fine cuisine, the hotel boasts two distinctive restaurants offering an enticing selection of dishes. Public rooms are spacious and delightfully furnished and service, in every aspect, is efficient and willing. Croquet and bowls may be played in the hotel's own grounds. ****.

BLACKSMITH'S ARMS HOTEL,
Hartoft, Rosedale, Pickering,
North Yorkshire YO18 8EN

Tel: 07515 331

Licensed; 14 bedrooms, all with private bathrooms; Historic interest; Car park (30); York 25 miles, Helmsley 16; ££.

Welcome to the Blacksmith's Arms Hotel, a charming sixteenth-century farmhouse that has been carefully restored and extended over the years to provide a hotel and restaurant of exceptional character. Cosy inglenooks, roaring open fires, original stonework and period furniture all combine to create an atmosphere of warmth, peace and seclusion. Dine sumptuously in our elegant restaurant; relax with an aperitif in the beamed cocktail bar; unwind in the luxury of your individually designed bedroom; explore the glorious countryside of Ryedale that lies right on your doorstep. At the Blacksmith's Arms Hotel, far from the madding crowd, your pleasure is our business. *ETB Commended, AA and RAC***.*

NORTH YORKSHIRE – RICH IN TOURIST ATTRACTIONS!

Dales, moors, castles, abbeys, cathedrals – you name it and you're almost sure to find it in North Yorkshire. Leading attractions include Castle Howard, the moorlands walks at Goathland, the Waterfalls at Falling Foss, Skipton, Richmond, Wensleydale, Bridestones Moor, Ripon Cathedral, Whitby, Settle and, of course, York itself.

Simonstone Hall

SIMONSTONE HALL,
Hawes,
North Yorkshire DL8 3LY

Tel: 0969 667255
Fax: 0969 667741

Licensed; 10 bedrooms, all with private bathrooms; Dogs welcome; Car park (24); Kendal 26 miles, Kirkby Lonsdale 23, Settle 22, Leyburn 16; £££.

Let yourself be pampered at Simonstone Hall, former home of the Earls of Wharncliffe, built in 1733. Its situation is rural but not isolated, being on the Buttertubs Pass just one-and-a-half miles from Hawes, England's highest market town. The fresh air of the countryside, the space, grace, comfort and good food make it ideal for relaxing and shedding the cares and pressures of modern day living. Our comfortable panelled drawing rooms, bar and all the main bedrooms face south with stunning views across Wensleydale. For a few days enjoy a leisurely pace of life, with fresh local produce being cooked to order, with vegetarian and healthy choice menus if you prefer, and an extensive list of wines from practically all corners of the world. Special short break terms are offered and during the cooler months the log fires offer a cheerful welcome on your return from your day out in the Dales. Dogs always welcome. ☙ ☙ ☙ *Commended, Winner of ETB's Warmest Hotelier and RAC Blue Ribbon Awards for the last 4 years.*

MANOR HOUSE FARM,
Ingleby Greenhow, Near Great Ayton,
North Yorkshire TS9 6RB

Tel: 0642 722384*

Residential licence; 3 bedrooms; Historic interest; Stokesley 4 miles; £.

This is a delightful stone-built farmhouse (part ca.1760) in the North York Moors National Park, idyllically set at the end of a half-mile wooded drive, adjacent to the ancient Manor. The accommodation is of the highest standard. Fine evening dinners are served by candlelight. Ideal for walking, touring and for nature lovers. Brochure on request. ☙ ☙ *Commended, AA, Les Routiers, Which Hotel Guide.*

MOORGARTH HALL COUNTRY HOUSE HOTEL,
New Road, Ingleton,
North Yorkshire LA6 3HL

Tel: 05242 41946

Fax: 05242 42252

Restaurant and residential licence; 8 bedrooms, all en suite; Dogs welcome by arrangement; Car park (14); Settle 9 miles, Kirkby Lonsdale 8; £.

Built in 1891 and set well back from the road in its own grounds of one-and-a-half acres, Moorgarth Hall, completely refurbished, combines the elegance and charm of a Victorian country house with all the requirements of a modern hotel. Henry and Liz Ibberson started in 1989, having decided to create the sort of hotel in which they themselves would wish to stay. The result offers their guests all the warmth and comfort of a traditional Yorkshire welcome, coupled with good wholesome cooking, with some interesting variations and a wine list to match. It is first and foremost their family home and you are made to feel very welcome within it. On the threshold of the Dales, within easy reach of the Lakes, and on the doorstep of the spectacular Ingleton Falls, not to mention the Three Peaks and show caves, Moorgarth Hall is ideally placed for short breaks at any time of year. *ETB* 👑 👑 👑 *Commended.*

GRASSFIELDS COUNTRY HOUSE HOTEL,
Wath Road, Pateley Bridge,
North Yorkshire HG3 5HL

Tel: 0423 711412*

Residential licence; 9 bedrooms, all with private bathrooms; Historic interest; Children and pets welcome; Car park (20); Harrogate 11 miles; £.

This handsome Georgian building, surrounded by lawns and trees and set in the heart of "Herriot" country, epitomises the elegance and charm of that bygone age, yet with an air of informality and friendliness that ensures a really relaxing stay. The spacious and comfortable bedrooms enjoy lovely garden and countryside views; all have en suite bathrooms and television. Free range eggs and fresh local produce, including trout from the River Nidd, are used in the preparation of traditional English dishes; packed lunches are provided on request and special and vegetarian diets can be catered for. Grassfields is a perfect base for touring the Dales and for visiting York and Harrogate. 👑 👑 👑 *Commended, AA **, Les Routiers.*

THE LODGE COUNTRY HOUSE HOTEL,
Middleton Road, Pickering,
North Yorkshire YO18 8NQ

Tel: 0751 72976

Fully licensed; 9 bedrooms, all with private bathrooms; Car park (15); Whitby 21 miles, York 18, Scarborough 16, Helmsley 14; ££.

A peaceful country house hotel secluded amidst three acres of lawns and terraces, The Lodge offers superb accommodation throughout. The delightful guest rooms are all en suite, with direct-dial telephone, hospitality trays and colour television. A charming bar and gracious drawing room both overlook the gardens. The lovely Victorian Conservatory Restaurant is the perfect setting in which to enjoy a delicious selection of both traditional and more adventurous cuisine, all prepared and presented to the highest possible standards. This delightful hotel is situated on the outskirts of Pickering, the natural centre from which to explore the North Yorkshire Moors, the Heritage Coast and historic York. 👑 👑 👑 👑 *Highly Commended.* **See also Colour Advertisement p.11.**

RAVEN HALL COUNTRY HOUSE HOTEL AND GOLF COURSE,
Ravenscar, Scarborough,
North Yorkshire YO13 0ET

Tel: 0723 870353
Fax: 0723 870072

Licensed; 53 bedrooms, all with private bathrooms; Historic interest; Children and pets welcome; Car park (200); Whitby 14 miles, Scarborough 10, Robin Hood's Bay 3; £££.

Standing dramatically on the cliffs 600 feet above sea level, with panoramic views of Robin Hood's Bay, this historic country house hotel is idyllically situated in 100 acres of North Yorkshire Moors parkland. It is convenient for all the tourist attractions of the area, including the lively resorts of Scarborough and Whitby. There is a wide range of entertainments and leisure activities for all the family in the extensive grounds, including a challenging 9-hole golf course, swimming pool and paddling pool, tennis courts, bowling green, clock golf, putting, giant chess, and croquet. Indoor facilities include a hair and beauty salon, sauna, two bars and a lounge with regular social events and party nights, a games room with billiards, snooker and table tennis, and a children's sports and leisure host (some creche facilities are available). Raven Hall is renowned for its excellent cuisine and the warmth of its Yorkshire hospitality. *RAC and AA***.*

HARTFORTH HALL HOTEL,
Gilling West, Richmond,
North Yorkshire DL10 5JU

Tel: 0748 825715
Fax: 0748 825781

Licensed; 8 bedrooms, 7 with private bathrooms; Historic interest; Children welcome; Car park (50); Richmond 3 miles; £.

A splendid country mansion, tastefully refurbished, in a splendid setting at the Gateway to the Dales. It is conveniently located just one mile from the A66, three miles from the A1 and just 15 minutes from Teesside Airport. Places of interest nearby include the Bowes and Beamish Museum and the Georgian Theatre at Richmond. Golf and walking Short Breaks.

EAST AYTON LODGE COUNTRY HOTEL,
Moor Lane, East Ayton, Scarborough,
North Yorkshire YO13 9EW

Tel: 0723 864227
Fax: 0723 862680

Residential and restaurant licence; 17 bedrooms, all with private bathrooms; Children and pets welcome; Car park (50); Scarborough 4 miles; ££.

Delightfully situated between the North Yorkshire Moors National Park and the popular resort of Scarborough, this magnificently appointed hotel offers the best of both worlds and also many attractions of its own. Close to the River Derwent, the hotel is set in tranquil grounds of 3 acres. The excellent restaurant provides the wherewithal to dine in elegant surroundings and enjoy the splendid English, French and vegetarian cuisine, much of the produce being home-grown. The dining room has a dance floor making it ideal for dinner dances and private functions. Guest rooms are furnished to a high standard; all have en suite facilities, colour television, radio/alarm, direct-dial telephone, central heating and numerous extras. There are also two honeymoon suites with traditional four-poster beds. *ETB* ✿ ✿ ✿ ✿, *Les Routiers.*

THE DEVONSHIRE ARMS COUNTRY HOUSE HOTEL,
Bolton Abbey, Skipton,
North Yorkshire BD23 6AJ

Tel: 0756 710441

Fax: 0756 710564

Fully licensed; 40 bedrooms, all with private bathroom; Historic interest; Car park; Leeds 26 miles, Harrogate 22; ££££.

Fine food and friendly, hospitable service await our guests at this renowned traditional country estate hotel in the Yorkshire Dales National Park. Bordering the lovely River Wharfe, within twelve acres of parkland, the hotel is set amidst some of the most breathtaking scenery in Britain. Many artists and writers, including Turner and the Bronte sisters, have been inspired by the rare beauty of the setting. Featuring log fires and four-poster bedrooms, fine furnishings and paintings from Chatsworth, the hotel interior has been stylishly decorated throughout under the personal supervision of the Duchess of Devonshire.

LARPOOL HALL COUNTRY HOUSE HOTEL,
Larpool Lane, Whitby,
North Yorkshire YO22 4ND

Tel and Fax: 0947 602737

Fully licensed; 14 bedrooms, all with private bathrooms; Historic interest; Children welcome; Car park (20); Scarborough 19 miles.

From the beautiful entrance hall with its original mahogany balustered staircase, past the columned Venetian window, the visitor to this elegant Georgian mansion is led to large, attractively decorated bedrooms with such splendid modern facilities as full en suite bathrooms, colour television, telephone and hospitality trays. Delightfully placed between the moors and the historic port and resort of Whitby, the present building was erected in 1796 on the site of the original manor. Transformed into a distinctive country hotel in 1986 by Keith and Electra Robinson, Larpool Hall overlooks the Esk Valley and is a tranquil holiday venue, one of its salient attractions being Electra's wide and expert knowledge of traditional English fare. 🏵 🏵 🏵 🏵 *Commended, AA **.*

West Yorkshire

HOLDSWORTH HOUSE HOTEL,
Holmfield, Halifax,
West Yorkshire HX2 9TG

Tel: 0422 240024*
Fax: 0422 245174

Fully licensed; 40 bedrooms, all with private bathrooms; Historic interest; Children welcome, pets allowed except in public areas; Car park (50); Bradford 7 miles; £££.

One does not immediately associate the hard-working town of Halifax with the opulence found at this historic house. However, it is fair to say that it was through industry that the house, now Grade II listed, was built in 1633. Transformed 30 years ago into a hotel of distinction, Holdsworth House is, in fact, three miles north of the town and as a base for exploration of the Bronte Country, Pennines and Dales or the commercial call of Leeds, Bradford or Huddersfield, there is no finer place in which to stay. Individually designed bedrooms all have bathrooms, remote-control colour television, radio and direct-dial telephone. The hotel is decorated with a wealth of oak and antiques, and the cuisine subject to constant recommendation. Specially equipped rooms are set aside for conferences and private functions. 🌷 🌷 🌷 🌷 *Highly Commended, AA ***.*

WOOD HALL,
Trip Lane, Linton, Near Wetherby,
West Yorkshire LS22 4JA

Tel: 0937 587271
Fax: 0937 584353

Restaurant and residential licence; 44 bedrooms, all with private bathrooms; Historic interest; Children and pets welcome; York 11 miles, Harrogate 10 miles, Wetherby 1; ££££.

The approach to Wood Hall through carefully tended parkland, over a stone bridge and then onto a wide sweep of terrace, fills one with a sense of pleasurable anticipation. One's immediate reaction on catching sight of this fine house is complete satisfaction, because here a Georgian mansion has been sensitively refurbished to create a country house hotel of unique charm and character. Bedrooms are of luxurious standard, and for that extra special occasion, suites with private sitting rooms and magnificent four-poster beds are available. Sumptuous soft furnishings, oak panelling and elegant decor in the public rooms, combined with attentive but unobtrusive service, put the final gloss on the excellent reputation Wood Hall has gained far beyond the borders of Yorkshire. Amenities include a leisure club with swimming pool, gymnasium etc. 🌷 🌷 🌷 🌷 🌷 *Highly Commended, AA Three Red Stars, RAC****, Egon Ronay 80%.*

Channel Islands

HOTEL HOUGUE DU POMMIER,
**Hougue du Pommier Road, Castel,
Guernsey, Channel Islands**

Tel: 0481 56531

Fax: 0481 56260

Fully licensed; 38 bedrooms, all with private bathrooms; Historic interest; Children welcome, guide dogs only; Car park (70); Jersey 25 miles; £.

The Hotel Hougue du Pommier (Apple Tree Hill) stands in 10 acres of grounds, only 10 minutes' walk from the sandy beaches of Grandes Rocques and Cobo. This elegant hotel, which has a full range of modern facilities, was once a farmhouse, and today the dining room incorporates the old cider room, parlour and bakery. Here an extensive à la carte menu is available nightly. Traditional furnishings create a warm and relaxed atmosphere, with tastefully appointed en suite bedrooms, all with colour television, radio, baby listening intercoms and direct-dial telephone. The hotel also has a sauna, solarium, games room, a solar heated swimming pool, 18-hole putting green, 10-hole pitch and putt golf course and a courtesy coach to and from St Peter Port. 10-rink indoor lawn bowling centre nearby. ♣ ♣ ♣ ♣, AA and RAC**, Ashley Courtenay Recommended.

The **£** symbol when appearing at the end of the italic section of an entry shows the anticipated price, during 1993, for a **single room with English Breakfast.**

Under £30	**£**	**Over £45 but under £60**	**£££**
Over £30 but under £45	**££**	**Over £60**	**££££**

This is meant as an indication only and does not show prices for Special Breaks, Weekends, etc. Guests are therefore advised to verify all prices on enquiring or booking.

LA GRANDE MARE HOTEL,
**Vazon Bay, Castel, Guernsey,
Channel Islands**

Tel: 0481 56576
Fax: 0481 56532

Fully licensed; 24 bedrooms, all with private bathrooms; Children welcome; Car park (200); St Peter Port 10 miles; ££££.

What a location! Set in 100 acres of its own private grounds with soporific views over the Atlantic Ocean, 100 yards from the sandy beach of Vazon Bay and just a short 15-minute drive from St Peter Port, La Grande Mare with its elegant surroundings is the ideal place for you to enjoy your holiday. Our accommodation ranges from four-poster double rooms to one and two bedroomed luxury penthouse suites with lounges, which are ideal for families. All rooms include en suite luxury bathroom, telephone, satellite television, snack or tea-making facilities; most rooms have balconies, ideal for watching the sun setting over the sea. A babysitting or listening service, together with laundry facilities and room service are also available. Relax and enjoy facilities which include golf, a coarse fishing lake, swimming pool and spa; just a short stroll across the bay and you can surf, sail, windsurf or jog. Qualified golf tuition is also available. Our European-style restaurant offers award-winning cuisine and a choice of table d'hôte and à la carte menus which are complemented by an extensive wine list, together with some of the finest ports and brandies in existence. Our high standards are maintained by highly trained, efficient and friendly staff. Country House hospitality, with Special Breaks throughout the year. ❧ ❧ ❧ ❧ ❧, *RAC**** and Merit Award 1991, Les Routiers Award for Excellence 1990/1/2, "Restaurant of the Year 1992" Ashley Courtenay Highly Recommended Hotel.*

CHATEAU LA CHAIRE,
**Rozel Bay, Jersey,
Channel Islands JE3 6AJ**

Tel: 0534 863354
Fax: 0534 865137

Residential and restaurant licence; 14 bedrooms, all with private bathrooms; Historic interest; Children over 7 years welcome, no pets in bedrooms or restaurant; Car park (30); £££.

Nestling on the slopes of the Rozel Valley, ablaze with floral colour all year round, this spaciously proportioned hotel provides magnificent accommodation in a dream setting. Furthermore, a reputation for excellent cuisine establishes the exciting menus to be amongst the very best in the island. Seafood is naturally a speciality but there are dishes to suit all tastes, adventurous or traditional. The hotel presents a delightful mixture of English virtues and French flair, especially in the restaurant. Only a few minutes' stroll will bring one to the bustling fishing harbour of Rozel Bay with its lovely beaches, whilst for duty free shopping, St. Helier is only a short drive away. Bedrooms are individually furnished to the highest possible standards with an impressive array of personal comforts. *Jersey Tourist Board ✿ ✿ ✿ ✿, ***.*

Clwyd

ABBEY GRANGE HOTEL,
Llangollen,
Clwyd LL20 8NN

Tel: 0978 860753

Fully licensed; 8 bedrooms, all with private bathrooms; Children welcome; Car park; Wrexham 9 miles; £.

Resting at the foot of the spectacular Horseshoe Pass, with magnificent views of fields and mountains to all sides, this family-run hotel offers an idyllic setting for your holiday, combining the character of an old country house with the comfort of modern amenities. Nearby is the thirteenth century Valle Crucis Abbey, and also the charming country town of Llangollen, venue of the famous International Musical Eisteddfod. All the spacious and well-appointed bedrooms are en suite and have colour television and tea/coffee making facilities. Catering is of a high standard, ranging from a comprehensive bar menu to full à la carte meals, with a good selection of fine wines. There are many places of interest in the area, including the spectacular Horseshoe Falls; Snowdonia National Park and the North Wales coastal resorts are within comfortable driving distance. *WTB* ♥ ♥ ♥.

NOTE

RUTHIN CASTLE,
Ruthin,
Clwyd LL15 2NU

Tel: 082-42 2664
Fax: 082-42 5978

Fully licensed; 58 bedrooms, all with private bathrooms; Historic interest; Children welcome;
Car park (200); Wrexham 14 miles; £££.

This noble and intriguing building dates from 1282 and stands in parklike grounds of 30 acres. Today, it offers distinguished accommodation for the discerning holidaymaker in a peaceful and beautiful setting. Indeed, every attempt has been made to halt the passage of time for, spanning the centuries from bygone days of chivalry, its traditional hospitality remains. Guests may enjoy the authentic flavour of medieval living at the banquets which are held regularly. At these occasions, one may quaff wine from pewter goblets, eat traditional dishes with a dagger and listen to harp music and singing by Ladies of the Court. Despite this emphasis on days of yore, guest rooms are equipped to the highest modern standards. *WTB* 🌸 🌸 🌸 🌸, ****, Two BTA "Come to Britain" Awards.*

Dyfed

THE MILL AT GLYNHIR,
Llandybie, Ammanford,
Dyfed SA18 2TE

Tel: 0269 850672*

Residential and restaurant licence; 11 bedrooms, all with private bathrooms; Historic interest;
Children over 11 years and pets welcome; Car park (20); Ammanford 2 miles; ££.

Built on the side of a valley with extensive views towards the Brecon Beacons National Park, the family-run Mill is at least 250 years old. Converted into a country hotel blessed with fine modern comforts, this is the ideal venue for those who really want to get away from it all. The only neighbours are the occupants of three cottages and the wildlife! The rewards are bountiful, the best of British cooking being paramount amongst them. The property adjoins the pretty Glynhir Golf Course (free to residents) and borders two acres of land by the River Loughor with its good trout fishing. There is a heated indoor pool and some of the bedrooms have direct access to a sun-bathing patio. *WTB* 🌸 🌸 🌸 🌸 *Commended.*

TREGYNON COUNTRY FARMHOUSE HOTEL,
Gwaun Valley, Near Fishguard,
Dyfed SA65 9TU

Tel: 0239 820531

Fax: 0239 820808

Restaurant and residential licence; 8 bedrooms, all with private bathrooms; Historic interest; Children welcome; Car park; Carmarthen 35 miles, Cardigan 19; £.

In the Pembrokeshire Coast National Park with superb views over the Gwaun Valley, this award-winning beamed sixteenth century farmhouse offers a country house holiday where lovers of good food will feel at home. Renowned for its traditional cuisine with wholefood and vegetarian specialities, as featured in "Here's Health", Tregynon uses fresh produce wherever possible, including its own trout. Virtually everything is made on the premises, including the oak-smoking of gammon and bacon using traditional methods, while sausages, breads, rolls and organic cheeses are made without additives. Accommodation is comfortable, and public rooms warm and cosy with log fires in winter. The grounds boast an Iron Age fort, 200 ft. waterfall, forest and wildlife. Two-day "Great Little Breaks" at special rates from November to Easter. *WTB* 🌸🌸🌸 *Highly Commended, RAC Highly Acclaimed, AA Selected, Ashley Courtenay Recommended.*

In the beautiful Ceiriog valley to the west of Chirk.

116   *Dyfed*

South Glamorgan

EGERTON GREY COUNTRY HOUSE HOTEL,
Porthkerry, Near Cardiff,
South Glamorgan CF6 9BZ

Tel: 0446 711666
Fax: 0446 711690

Restaurant licence; 10 bedrooms, all with private bathrooms; Historic interest; Car park; Cardiff 10 miles; DB&B ££/£££.

A recommended centre from which to explore the lovely and uncrowded Gower Peninsula and the Brecon Beacons, this stylish and distinguished country house was opened as a small and luxurious hotel as recently as 1988. Only 10 miles from Cardiff, it is set in a secluded, wooded valley in seven acres of gardens, with views down to Porthkerry Park and the sea. The excellent facilities accorded guests include exquisitely furnished bedrooms (all with private bathrooms), two dining rooms, library and magnificent Edwardian drawing room. Within the grounds is an all-weather tennis court and also a croquet lawn. Only a short stroll away is a well-maintained country park with an 18-hole pitch and putt course. The cuisine is outstanding and dining here by candlelight is a memorable experience. Recommended by all hotel and restaurant guides. *WTB* 🌸🌸🌸🌸 *Highly Commended, "Taste of Wales" Cuisine Award.*

Please mention
Recommended COUNTRY HOTELS
when seeking refreshment or
accommodation at a Hotel
mentioned in these pages

West Glamorgan

NICHOLASTON HOUSE HOTEL,
Nicholaston, Swansea,
West Glamorgan SA3 2HL

Tel: 0792 371317

Hotel and restaurant licence; 11 bedrooms, all with private bathrooms; Children welcome, pets by arrangement; Car park (35); Swansea 15 miles; £/££.

Enjoying one of the finest situations in the glorious Gower, famed for its quiet sandy beaches, this well recommended hotel has beautiful grounds from which there is a superb panorama across the Bristol Channel to the Devon coast. A refreshing place in which to stay, the hotel, so pleasantly run by the Lewis family, has excellent accommodation, all guest rooms having private amenities, colour television and tea and coffee making facilities and, of course, wonderful views. The day starts with a full 'English' breakfast and on return from a day's activities, there is the promise of a memorable dinner chosen from the table d'hôte or extensive à la carte menu. Relaxing moments may be spent in the bar or snooker room or just sitting outside on the garden terrace. *WTB ☙ ☙ ☙, AA/RAC**, Taste of Wales.*

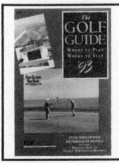

Gwent

WYE VALLEY HOTEL,
Tintern, Near Chepstow,
Gwent NP6 6SP

Tel: 0291 689441
Fax: 0291 684440

Fully licensed; 9 bedrooms, all with private shower or bathroom; Children welcome; Car park (50); Chepstow 6 miles; £/££.

The Wye Valley Hotel is a friendly hostelry of great charm. All rooms have en suite facilities, four-poster or half-tester beds, colour television, direct-dial telephone, hairdryers and tea/coffee making equipment. Our chefs offer bar meals, grill menu, à la carte and weekend carvery, all at reasonable prices and freshly prepared on the premises. The public bar offers a selection of real ales. Special Breaks available. *WTB* 🌷🌷🌷🌷, *Les Routiers.*

PLEASE ENCLOSE A STAMPED ADDRESSED ENVELOPE WHEN WRITING TO ENQUIRE ABOUT ACCOMMODATION FEATURED IN THIS GUIDE

Gwynedd

TREFEDDIAN HOTEL,
Aberdovey,
Gwynedd LL35 0SB

Tel: 0654 767213*

Licensed; 46 bedrooms, all with private bathrooms; Children and dogs welcome; Car park (40), garage (20); Aberystwyth 29 miles; DB&B £££.

The Trefeddian Hotel is a family owned and run hotel with a magnificent view overlooking golf links, sandy beach and Cardigan Bay. Facilities include an indoor heated swimming pool, snooker table, table tennis and games room. A hard tennis court is also available, and a nine-hole pitch and putt course. Water sports facilities are also available on the estuary of the River Dovey. The bedrooms are well-equipped, with colour television, radio, baby listening service, telephone and central heating. The hotel is an ideal centre for touring Snowdonia National Park and for visiting the RSPB bird reserve, and the Tal-y-Llyn narrow gauge railway. Colour brochure forwarded with pleasure. *WTB* 🌷 🌷 🌷 🌷*, AA and RAC***, Egon Ronay Recommended.*

BERTHLWYD HALL HOTEL,
Llechwedd, Near Conwy,
Gwynedd LL32 8DQ

Tel: 0492 592409
Fax: 0492 572290

Fully licensed; 8 bedrooms, all with private bathrooms; Historic interest; Children and pets welcome; Car park (50); Conwy 2 miles; £££.

Maintained in grandiose Victorian style in concert with the opulence of the period, this lovely manor house hotel has wonderful views of the Conwy Valley and Castle across green fields. It is only a mile from the old town and the surroundings vary from verdant, with the famous Bodnant Gardens nearby, to the true majesty of Snowdonia. Splendid oak panelling, a magnificent galleried landing and staircase, carved fireplaces and stained glass windows all exert their influences on the relaxed atmosphere. The luxurious accommodation, kindly service, bar, games room and, last but not least, the excellence of the French-orientated Truffles Restaurant, will assure a holiday long to be cherished. *WTB* 🌷 🌷 🌷 *Highly Commended, Johansens, Ashley Courtenay Recommended.*

CASTELL CIDWM HOTEL,
Betws Garmon, Caernarvon,
Gwynedd LL54 7YT

Tel: 0286 85243

Licensed; 8 bedrooms, all with private bathrooms; Children welcome; Car park; Caernarvon 5 miles; £.

In one of the most beautiful settings in Wales on the south side of Snowdon, this delightfully tranquil lakeside hotel offers magnificent views of mountain, forest and water. Private trout fishing, boating and water sports are available from the hotel, with walking, climbing and pony trekking nearby. The hotel offers warm friendly hospitality, eight bedrooms (all en suite), a cosy bar, a bistro snack bar and an à la carte restaurant with a subtly different cuisine. Two and three day breaks available. *WTB* 🌷 🌷 🌷 *Commended, AA**.* **See also Colour Advertisement p.13.**

BODYSGALLEN HALL,
Llandudno,
Gwynedd LL30 1RS

Tel: 0492 584466
Fax: 0492 582519

Fully licensed; 28 bedrooms, all with private bathrooms; Historic interest; Children over 8 years welcome, pets in cottage suites only; Car park (70); Colwyn Bay 4½ miles; ££££.

Sympathetically restored, this imposing 17th century country house combines the elegance of a sedate past with twentieth-century comforts. Antiques and fine pictures charm the eye and each of the comfortable guest rooms has its own Edwardian-style bathroom, colour television, direct-dial telephone and electric trouser press. The house stands in delightful terraced grounds, the setting for several well furnished cottage suites with spectacular views of Snowdonia. This is the ideal centre for those wishing to get away from it all amidst majestic and peaceful surroundings yet with the amenities of a modern resort nearby. Special mention must be made of the cuisine with the imaginative "Bill of Fare", changed daily, featuring a number of unusual specialities as well as superbly-presented traditional dishes. 🌷 🌷 🌷 🌷 🌷 *Highly Commended, AA 3 Red Stars, RAC Blue Ribbon, Welsh Rarebits Member.*

GOGARTH ABBEY HOTEL,
West Shore, Llandudno,
Gwynedd LL30 2QY

Tel: 0492 876211

Fully licensed; 40 bedrooms, all with private bathrooms; Historic interest; Children and pets welcome; Car park; Bangor 19 miles, Colwyn Bay 4; ££.

Although set on Llandudno's West Shore, this superbly appointed hotel really comes into the country house category, standing as it does in its own spacious grounds, with views of Snowdonia and the Isle of Anglesey. It was here that Charles Dodgson, immortalised as Lewis Carroll, was inspired to write "Alice in Wonderland" for the owner's daughter. Today the attractive restaurant is the setting for imaginative and creative cuisine made even more enjoyable by attentive service. There are four beautifully appointed lounges and a pleasant cocktail bar. The tastefully decorated bedrooms all have private facilities, colour television, radio, direct-dial telephone and tea and coffee makers. For relaxation there is a heated indoor swimming pool with a games area, a putting green and a croquet lawn; dry-ski slope and two golf courses within easy reach. 🌷🌷🌷🌷, ***.

MINFFORDD HOTEL,
Talyllyn, Tywyn,
Gwynedd LL36 9AJ

Tel: 0654 761665*
Fax: 0654 761517

Residential and restaurant licence; 6 bedrooms, all with private bathrooms; Historic interest; Car park (12); Machynlleth 10 miles; DB&B (double) £££.

At last — an opportunity to escape and rediscover lost values set to flight by modern living. At the head of the remote and beautiful Dysynni Valley, this former coaching inn is a scenic gem in itself. Homely, warm and comfortable, the hotel is full of character. Guest rooms are tastefully furnished and each is centrally heated and has private bath and toilet facilities. Beauty spots and places of interest abound in the area, part of the dramatic patterns woven by mountains and streams, Talyllyn Lake, the famous Talyllyn Railway, Cader Idris, Dolgoch Falls amongst them. Always on one's return is the prospect of a sumptuous dinner and the recounting of the day's adventures before a log fire. 🌷🌷🌷🌷, *AA Red Star, RAC Blue Ribbon.*

Powys

CAER BERIS MANOR HOTEL,
Builth Wells,
Powys LD2 3NP

Tel: 0982 552601

Fax: 0982 552586

Fully licensed; 22 bedrooms, all with private bathrooms; Historic interest; Children and pets welcome; Car park (50); Brecon 14 miles; ££.

Offering superb modern facilities in a beautiful and unspoilt setting to which the magnificently appointed Caer Beris contributes with its own 27 acres of parkland, this is a delightful retreat for guests of all ages. Family action holidays are organised on a regular basis with play-leaders and instructors taking younger children on trips, whilst older children go on practical nature walks. Golfing and fishing packages may also be arranged for adults and facilities for shooting and pony trekking are available nearby. However, there are plenty of opportunities for passive relaxation at this most comfortable hotel which dates back to pre-Elizabethan times, and the cuisine, which covers a wide spectrum of tastes, is worthy of an accolade on its own account. *WTB* 🌸 🌸 🌸 🌸, ***.

TY CROESO HOTEL,
The Dardy, Llangattock, Crickhowell,
Powys NP8 1PU

Tel: 0873 810573

Licensed; 8 bedrooms, all with private bathrooms; Historic interest; Abergavenny 6 miles; ££.

Ty Croeso is in the Brecon Beacons National Park, set high on the hillside, with magnificent views over the Usk Valley to the Black Mountains. The gardens and terrace also overlook the valley. The hotel is ideally suited for walking, visiting places of interest in South and Mid Wales, and all outdoor activities. Originally part of a Victorian workhouse, it is now tastefully refurbished to provide comfort and every convenience for its guests. Log fires, stone walls and good music echo the traditional charm of the building. The standard of accommodation is high, but at realistic prices. The restaurant is renowned for its excellent food; an interesting A la Carte menu with traditional favourites is available. The "Tastes of Wales" menu, popular with locals as well as visitors, is different but delicious. "Ty Croeso", pronounced "Tee Croyso", translated means "House of Welcome", and you can be sure of a warm welcome from Kate and Peter Jones and their staff. *WTB* 🌸 🌸 🌸 *Highly Commended, AA**.* **See also Colour Advertisement p.13.**

If you've found
RECOMMENDED COUNTRY HOTELS
of service please tell your friends

LLANGOED HALL,
Llyswen, Brecon,
Powys LD3 0YP

Tel: 0874 754525

Fax: 0874 754545

Fully licensed; 23 bedrooms, all with private bathrooms; Historic interest; Children over 8 years welcome, kennels available for dogs; Car park (100); Brecon 9 miles; ££££.

This superb house on the banks of the lovely River Wye has its origins in 1632 when it was built on the foundations of an ancient grange. Redesigned in 1912, incorporating the beautiful Jacobean porch on the south wing, the elegant Llangoed Hall stands in delightful and well-established grounds and now welcomes guests into its exclusive Edwardian country house atmosphere. Grace and gentility mix easily with warm hospitality and opulent comforts. Spacious communal rooms, such as the Great Hall, library, morning and dining rooms, are furnished with impeccable taste and an eye for harmonious colour schemes; a great carved staircase climbs to an imposing, pillared picture gallery and thence to the splendid guest rooms, all of which have a private bathroom, television, radio and direct-dial telephone. A valet service operates from 8 a.m. to 10 p.m. Under the supervision of an artistic and skilled chef, the cuisine is delicately classical with emphasis on such delicacies as local game, Welsh lamb and Wye salmon and there is an enthralling selection of wines to complement each delicious meal. Gentle diversion may be sought playing cards or snooker in the library and more active pursuits to be enjoyed in the extensive grounds include tennis on an all-weather court and croquet. Pony trekking and good golf are available nearby. *WTB* 👑 👑 👑 👑 👑, *AA and RAC ****, Egon Ronay De Luxe Rating, Taste of Wales 1991.*

Angus

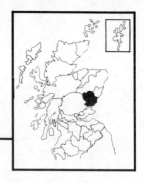

THE OLD MANSION HOUSE HOTEL, Auchterhouse, By Dundee, Angus DD3 0QN

Tel: 082-626 366*

Fax: 082-626 400

Fully licensed; 6 bedrooms, all with private bathrooms; Children and pets welcome; Car park (50); Dundee 6 miles; ££££.

Skilfully converted into a small luxury hotel, this interesting 16th century former baronial home now presents superb accommodation and is also highly regarded for its cuisine, wines and efficient service under the benign supervision of Owners, Nigel and Eva Bell. Each guest room is delightfully appointed with bathroom en suite, telephone and television and is centrally heated. The house has been in the ownership of several noted families and improvements made in the 17th century include the ornate plasterwork in the original drawing room with its Jacobean open fire, whilst the vaulted entrance hall is reminiscent of an earlier period. Sporting facilities in the 10-acre grounds are a squash court, heated swimming pool and croquet and tennis lawns. *AA*** and Rosette, Egon Ronay, Good Hotel Guide.*

FOR THE MUTUAL GUIDANCE OF GUEST AND HOST

Every year literally thousands of holidays, short-breaks and overnight stops are arranged through our guides, the vast majority without any problems at all. In a handful of cases, however, difficulties do arise about bookings, which often could have been prevented from the outset.

It is important to remember that when accommodation has been booked, both parties — guests and hosts — have entered into a form of contract. We hope that the following points will provide helpful guidance.

GUESTS: When enquiring about accommodation, be as precise as possible. Give exact dates, numbers in your party and the ages of any children. State the number and type of rooms wanted and also what catering you require — bed and breakfast, full board, etc. Make sure that the position about evening meals is clear — and about pets, reductions for children or any other special points.

Read our reviews carefully to ensure that the proprietors you are going to contact can supply what you want. Ask for a letter confirming all arrangements, if possible.

If you have to cancel, do so as soon as possible. Proprietors do have the right to retain deposits and under certain circumstances to charge for cancelled holidays if adequate notice is not given and they cannot re-let the accommodation.

HOSTS: Give details about your facilities and about any special conditions. Explain your deposit system clearly and arrangements for cancellations, charges, etc, and whether or not your terms include VAT.

If for any reason you are unable to fulfil an agreed booking without adequate notice, you may be under an obligation to arrange alternative suitable accommodation or to make some form of compensation.

While every effort is made to ensure accuracy, we regret that FHG Publications cannot accept responsibility for errors, omissions or misrepresentation in our entries or any consequences thereof. Prices in particular should be checked because we go to press early. We will follow up complaints but cannot act as arbiters or agents for either party.

Argyll

FALLS OF LORA HOTEL,
Connel Ferry, By Oban,
Argyll PA37 1PB

Tel: 0631-71 483
Fax: 0631-71 694

Fully licensed; 30 bedrooms, all with private bathrooms; Children and pets welcome; Car park (40); Oban 5 miles; ££.

Warm and welcoming, this fine Victorian hotel, overlooking Loch Etive, is beautifully furnished and appointed and offers guests of all ages the assurance of comfort and service. The local scenery is magnificent and the hotel is an ideal centre for touring, sailing, water-skiing, diving, fishing, pony trekking and gliding; and always the promise of good refreshment and company on one's return to base. Breakfasts and dinners are, to say the least, hugely appetising and there is a unique cocktail bar adjoining and a bistro where informal meals are served. All bedrooms have television, telephone and radio intercom with baby-listening available during office hours. Children sharing with two adults are offered free accommodation with only food charged for. 🌑🌑🌑 *Commended, AA and RAC **, Ashley Courtenay Recommended.*

The **£** symbol when appearing at the end of the italic section of an entry shows the anticipated price, during 1993, for a **single room with English Breakfast.**

Under £30	£	**Over £45 but under £60**	£££
Over £30 but under £45	££	**Over £60**	££££

This is meant as an indication only and does not show prices for Special Breaks, Weekends, etc. Guests are therefore advised to verify all prices on enquiring or booking.

ROCKHILL FARM COUNTRY HOUSE,
Ardbrecknish, By Dalmally,
Argyll PA33 1BH

Tel: 08663 218

Residential licence; 5 bedrooms, all with private bathrooms; Children over 10 years welcome; Inveraray 11 miles; DB&B ££.

Completely secluded half a mile down a farm track, this is an ideal spot for those wanting real peace and quiet. The only sound is the buzzards calling as they circle overhead, and the fields and woods around the house are home to otters, foxes, roe and red deer. This is a Hanoverian horse stud, with lots of mares and foals; black Welsh Mountain sheep are also kept. Some guests return year after year to enjoy the comfortable, informal, cottage-style accommodation and the highly acclaimed home cooking. We have 1100 yards of private lochshore trout and coarse fishing and a private lochan — a boat can be hired or bring your own. This is a superb area for birdwatching, walking, climbing and touring many castles and gardens — or just relaxing and enjoying the spectacular views. *AA and RAC Recommended.*

Ayrshire

ARDSTINCHAR HOTEL,
Main Street, Ballantrae, Near Girvan,
Ayrshire KA26 0NB

Tel: 046-583 254

Licensed; 4 bedrooms, all with showers; Children welcome; Girvan 12 miles; £.

Renowned for personal, friendly service and excellent food, the Ardstinchar Hotel is situated in a picturesque small village, close to the sea and ideal for golf, fishing and hill walking. Other activities available locally include horse riding, bowling and putting, and there is a bird sanctuary nearby. All the comfortable bedrooms have showers and washbasins, and accommodation is available at most reasonable rates, with reductions for children. **See also Colour Advertisement p.14.**

MONTGREENAN MANSION HOUSE HOTEL,
Montgreenan Estate, Near Kilwinning,
Ayrshire KA13 7QZ

Tel: 0294 57733

Fax: 0294 85397

Hotel licence; 21 bedrooms, all with private bathrooms; Historic interest; Children welcome, pets by arrangement; Car park (50); Irvine 4 miles; ££££.

We were faintly amused at the item on the dinner menu which read "Selection *oof* fresh vegetables and potatoes" but having soldiered valiantly through the magnificent courses one by one, we came to the opinion that it was not a misprint after all! Wonderful food, beautifully presented and reasonably priced. However, the joys of this grand early Victorian mansion extend well beyond the pleasures of the table. Delightfully furnished in keeping with its opulent origins and with modern conveniences skilfully introduced, the time-honoured appeal of this elegant country house remains undiminished. Bedrooms are appointed to de luxe standard with antique and reproduction furniture and a choice of sumptuous beds including a kingsize round bed and four-posters. Two bedroom suites have jacuzzis and all have colour television, radio, direct-dial telephone, private bar, tea-making facilities and many other useful items and room service. Guests return again and again to be spoilt in such a peaceful setting; to stroll through the 45 acres of gardens and woods, with distant views of lonely Ailsa Craig and the Arran Hills is a joy in itself. As a centre for Burns Country with, maybe, a few rounds on a variety of golf courses for which Ayrshire is noted, there can be no finer place. There are several rooms set aside for social functions and/or business meetings. ❦ ❦ ❦ ❦ *Highly Commended; AA and RAC***, Egon Ronay.*

Edinburgh & Lothians

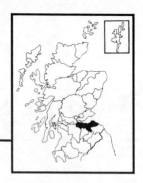

OLD ORIGINAL ROSLIN INN,
4 Main Street, Roslin,
Midlothian EH25 9LE

Tel: 031-440 2384

Fully licensed; 6 bedrooms, all with private bathrooms; Historic interest; Car park; Loanhead 2 miles; £.

The Old Original was in former times a temperance hotel, but those seeking liquid refreshment may be assured that today all four bars are well stocked with good beers, spirits and a most acceptable selection of fine wines. Substantial lunches and suppers are served in the comfortable lounge, and the à la carte menu attracts locals, as well as residents and passing trade, to the well laid out dining room which is graced by an interesting collection of antiques. Six bedrooms are available for letting, including a special honeymoon room, and all have pleasing decor, duvets and central heating.

A typical view of Edinburgh Castle.

Inverness-shire

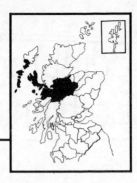

CORROUR HOUSE HOTEL,
Inverdruie, Aviemore,
Inverness-shire PH22 1QH　　　　　Tel: 0479 810220*

Residential/restricted licence; 8 bedrooms, all with private bathrooms; Children and dogs welcome; Car park (15); Aviemore one mile; ££.

For true Highland hospitality, peace, good food and ease of accessibility to the many leisure activities in the Spey Valley, this attractive hotel is the complete answer. Tastefully furnished, Corrour House stands in 4 acres of secluded garden and woodland adjacent to the Rothiemurchus Forest with wonderful views stretching to the Cairngorms. The hotel exudes the elegant charm of a bygone age although there is nothing archaic about the facilities available, the en suite rooms being beautifully appointed. The table d'hôte menu, changed daily, features prime Scottish beef, venison, salmon, trout and locally-caught game. Relaxation is an easily acquired state here and a cocktail bar, library and drawing room with a log fire contribute to a feeling of utter contentment. 🦢 🦢 🦢 🦢 *Highly Commended.*

HIGHLAND REGION — AND THE ISLANDS TOO!

From the genteel town of Inverness to the ragged formations of the west coast and on, over the sea to Skye and many more islands — yes Highland Region is vast! You'll probably not find that many people but places that most definitely should be found include the Caledonian Canal, Culloden, Mallaig, Loch Ness, Inverewe, Duncansby Head, Ben Nevis, the Cairngorms, Golspie, and the Islands themselves.

COZAC LODGE,
Glencannich, By Beauly,
Inverness-shire IV4 7LX

Tel: 04565 263

Restaurant and residential licence; 7 bedrooms, all with private bathrooms; Historic interest; Children welcome, pets by arrangement; Car park (12); Inverness 30 miles; £/££.

Warm and friendly and of great character, this one-time shooting lodge lies in the heart of the Highlands in Glen Cannich, famous for its red deer and other interesting wildlife. The situation is both tranquil and spectacular, and the views across Loch Sealbanach to the Affric Mountains are breathtaking. A country home in the truest sense, the hotel has comfortable lounges and luxuriously appointed guest rooms, each with its own bath or shower, WC and colour television. The tangy Highland air promotes healthy appetites which are well satisfied by the first-class and interesting cuisine, much use being made of fresh local produce in company with carefully selected wines. ♥ ♥ ♥ *Commended, AA**.*

THE LODGE ON THE LOCH,
Creag Dhu, Onich, By Fort William,
Inverness-shire PH33 6RY

Tel: 08553 237
Fax: 08553 463

Licensed; 20 bedrooms, 18 with private bathrooms; Children and dogs welcome; Car park (25); Edinburgh 120 miles, Glasgow 93, Oban 39; Fort William 10, Ballachulish 3; ££/£££.

The Lodge On The Loch enjoys one of the most romantic and spectacular lochside settings, in a land famed for its splendid scenery. Visitors to this lovely spot will enjoy a really warm Highland welcome, where old world standards of hospitality unite with modern comforts to ensure a restful, peaceful stay. All bedrooms are individually designed and furnished, and feature fine woven fabrics from the Islands, while the public rooms are cheered by log fires. The hotel is justly proud of its fine Highland cuisine, with local seafood, salmon, trout and venison; or you may care to try the wholefood vegetarian menu and irresistible home baking. *Recommmended by leading food and accommodation guides; STB* ♥ ♥ ♥ ♥ *Highly Commended.*

ALLT-NAN-ROS HOTEL,
Onich, By Fort William,
Inverness-shire PH33 6RY

Tel: 085-53 210*

Fax: 085-53 462

Licensed; 21 bedrooms, all with private bathrooms; Children and dogs welcome; Car park (50); Oban 39 miles, Fort William 10; ££.

Named in Gaelic after the cascading stream that runs through the beautiful and colourful four acres of gardens, this fine hotel will hold special appeal for lovers of wild and romantic mountain and loch scenery. Situated on the A82 in the crofting village of Onich, Allt-nan-Ros is an imposing building of Victorian origin that has been modernised with skill and imagination. Guest rooms have magnificent views, and are appointed with private bath and toilet facilities, radio, central heating, electric blankets and tea and coffee makers. Under the attentive care of an expert chef, the cuisine is superbly prepared and presented, from the full Scottish breakfast to dinner which features many imaginative specialities. *STB* 🌸 🌸 🌸 🌸 *Commended, Egon Ronay, Good Hotel Guide Recommended.*

DRUIMANDARROCH HOUSE,
Spean Bridge, Near Fort William,
Inverness-shire PH34 4EU

Tel: 039-781 335

Residential licence; 7 bedrooms, 2 with private facilities; Children and pets welcome; Car park (10); Fort William 10 miles; £.

"Druimandarroch House" is a small, personally run hotel which stays small to ensure you get personal service. We are ideally situated for carefree days of touring, coming back to dinner or a basket meal and a drink. All rooms have colour television and tea/coffee making facilities. There is a golf course nearby. Inflation Beaters — 1991 prices throughout 1993 at "Druimandarroch". We look forward to welcoming you. 🌸 🌸 *Approved.* **See also Colour Advertisement p.14.**

Isle of Mull

LINNDHU COUNTRY HOUSE HOTEL,
Tobermory,
Isle of Mull PA75 6QB

Tel: 0688 2425
Fax: 0688 2140

Restricted licence; 8 bedrooms, 5 with private bathrooms; Children and pets welcome; Car park (20); Tobermory 2 miles; £/££££.

Jennifer and Ian McLean offer you a warm welcome at Linndhu. Set in 35 acres of woodland and beautiful gardens, with magnificent views over the Sound of Mull, this traditional Highland hotel brings you superb comfort and imaginative, delicious cuisine. A trout stream flows through the grounds, and we can arrange river, loch and sea fishing. Maybe you'll want to walk, golf, birdwatch, deerstalk, or just relax and enjoy the island's spectacular scenery — the choice is yours. We are just two miles south of Tobermory on the A848 Salen to Tobermory road. ♣ ♣ ♣ *Commended.* **See also Colour Advertisement p.15.**

Isle of Raasay

ISLE OF RAASAY HOTEL,
Isle of Raasay,
By Kyle of Lochalsh IV40 8PB

Tel: 047-862 222/226*

Licensed; 12 bedrooms, all with private bathrooms; Parking (12); Isle of Skye (ferry) 15 mins.

The hotel is situated in a woodland garden with breathtaking views of the sea and the famous Cuillin Mountains of Skye. The unspoilt Isle of Raasay is easily reached by car ferry from the Isle of Skye and offers much of interest to geologists, botanists, birdwatchers, naturalists, fishermen and hillwalkers. The hotel's comfortable bedrooms all have private bathrooms, tea-making facilities, colour television, radio, and individually controlled central heating. Proprietor, Mrs Isobel Nicolson, aims to provide the best of good, wholesome, fresh food, with delicious home-made soups and sweets as specialities. This peaceful island is ideal for a relaxing holiday, with the added pleasures of modern comforts in a family-run hotel.

Morayshire

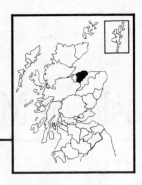

KNOCKOMIE HOTEL,
Grantown Road, Forres,
Morayshire IV36 0SG

Tel: 0309 673146

Fax: 0309 673290

Fully licensed; 7 bedrooms, all with private bathrooms; Historic interest; Children and pets welcome; Car park (40); Inverness 27 miles, Elgin 12; £££.

An attractive country hotel of good solid worth, the appeal of Knockomie is primarily to anglers, golfers, tourists, businessmen and those who appreciate fine malt whiskies. Accommodation is also well ordered and the Resident Director, Gavin Ellis, backed by a courteous and efficient staff, goes out of his way to ensure the well-being of guests to this rewarding corner of Scotland. Activity holidays may be arranged, tailored to guests' requirements which may also cover golf, fishing, walking and pony trekking. The guest rooms are particularly well appointed, each having a private bathroom, colour television, clock radio/alarm, direct-dial telephone and tea and coffee-making facilities. For that special occasion (or special person), a romantic 'champagne break' may make dreams come true. ♣ ♣ ♣ ♣ *Commended, Taste of Scotland, Ashley Courtenay.*

Perthshire

KIRKSIDE HOUSE HOTEL,
Glenisla, By Blairgowrie,
Perthshire PH11 8PH

Tel: 057-582 278

Fully licensed; 6 bedrooms, one with private bathroom; Historic interest; Children and pets welcome; Car park (20); Blairgowrie 20 miles; £.

This little gem of a country hotel was, as its name suggests, an 18th century manse. A listed building of great charm and presence, the hotel stands in tranquil surroundings in 1½ acres of gardens and is a wonderful centre for tours of the Central Highlands with the region's fascinating flora and fauna and excellent opportunities for hill walking, pony trekking, golf, fishing and shooting. For a peaceful and revivifying holiday, this homely venue on the upper reaches of the River Isla is to be recommended. Comfortable accommodation is available for 12 guests with in-house relaxation to be found communing with new-found friends in the bar/games room or watching colour television in the residents' lounge. 👑 👑.

KINLOCH HOUSE HOTEL,
By Blairgowrie,
Perthshire PH10 6SG

Tel: 025 0884 237
Fax: 025 0884 333

Fully licensed; 21 bedrooms, all with private bathrooms; Children welcome, pets by arrangement; Car park (35); Dundee 17 miles; £££.

Victorian in origin but extended in 1911, this is a fine example of a Scottish country house which stands in 25 acres of woods and parkland grazed by Highland cattle. With far-reaching views and superbly placed in the Perthshire Highlands, the hotel is ideally situated for country pursuits, yet the main urban centres, and even the coast, are within easy reach. Nearby, there is great trout and salmon fishing, shooting and golf as well as superb walking terrain and many historic houses to visit. The hotel has its own Sportsman's Room complete with drying facilities, gun cupboard, game larder, etc. On a more relaxed (or, maybe, more comfortable note) guest rooms are furnished and decorated to the very highest standards; all have private amenities, some with four-poster or half-tester beds. The cuisine at this warm and restful retreat will cap a pleasure-spent day with the menu offering an extensive selection of classic and traditional Scottish dishes for which many accolades have been received. Golden moments of delightful anticipation, studying the possibilities of the menu in the cocktail bar, will presage a memorable meal. David and Sarah Shentall are to be complimented on the organisation and standards of service at this happy and distinguished hotel which must rank high on the list of recommendations for a true Scottish vacation. ❀ ❀ ❀ ❀ *Highly Commended, AA Hospitality Award 1991, Good Hotel Guide "Cesar" Award 1991.*

POPPIES HOTEL,
Leny Road, Callander,
Perthshire FK17 8AL

Tel: 0877 30329*

Fully licensed; 11 bedrooms, 7 with private bathrooms; Children welcome; Car park (16); Stirling 16 miles; £.

Callander is an attractive town in the heart of the Trossachs and Rob Roy Country and pleasantly situated in its West End, Poppies offers splendid accommodation, comfort and hospitality. It is only a few minutes' walk to the banks of the River Teith and the Callander Crags, whilst the famous Bracklinn Fells are only a short distance away as well as opportunities for golf, fishing, pony trekking and water sports. Most of the guest rooms have bath or shower en suite and all have colour television, radio, telephone, central heating and tea and coffee-making facilities. In the matter of cuisine, the hotel's renowned Poppies Restaurant lures knowledgeable diners from a wide area to enjoy, by candlelight, international specialities from an extensive à la carte menu.

KEPPOCH HOUSE HOTEL,
Perth Road, Crieff,
Perthshire PH7 3EQ

Tel: 0764 4341*
Fax: 0764 5435

Licensed; 6 bedrooms, 5 with private bathrooms; Children and pets welcome; Perth 16 miles; £/££.

This charming hotel is located on the Perth road, only ten minutes' walk from the centre of Crieff. Situated within its own grounds and having a south-facing aspect, its location offers beautiful views of the Vale of Strathearn and the imposing Ochil Hills. After an enjoyable day on one of the many golf courses or fishing rivers or lochs in this area, relax in comfortable surroundings and enjoy an evening meal prepared from fresh local produce. ♥ ♥ ♥ Approved. **See also Colour Advertisement p.15.**

BIRNAM HOTEL,
Birnam, Dunkeld,
Perthshire PH8 0BQ

Tel: 0350 727462
Fax: 0350 728979

Hotel licence; 28 bedrooms, all with private bathrooms; Historic interest; Children and pets welcome; Car park (20); Perth 15 miles, Pitlochry 13; ££.

In true Scottish baronial style, this impressively decorated hotel stands on the south bank of the River Tay opposite Dunkeld, the ancient capital of Scotland. A driveway from the hotel leads to the Birnam Oak, the last remnant of the Birnam Woods, made famous in Shakespeare's 'Macbeth'. Apart from its splendid ambience, there is nothing historic about the appointments awaiting the guest of today. Bedrooms are, for the most part, spacious and are superbly furnished, all having private facilities, colour television, telephone and tea and coffee tray. An attractive cocktail bar is a popular meeting place and the Lodge Grill Room, also open to non-residents, offers a superb table d'hôte menu. A magnificent baronial dining hall is a suitably imposing setting for conferences and private functions. *AA and RAC***.*

MORENISH LODGE HIGHLAND HOUSE HOTEL,
By Killin,
Perthshire FK21 8TX

Tel: 056-72 258*

Restricted licence; 13 bedrooms, all with private bathrooms; Children over 4 years welcome; Car park (18); Crianlarich 14 miles; £.

Dating from the mid-18th century and formerly the shooting lodge of the Earl of Breadalbane, this lovely Highland hotel sits 200 feet above Loch Tay enjoying views that soon make one forget the rush and tear of city life. Guest rooms are extremely well appointed, all having private facilities and carefully restricted numbers ensures that each guest has the personal attention of Proprietors, Graeme and Maureen Naylor. Varied traditional cuisine is served in a pleasant dining room with picture windows overlooking the loch and for relaxation guests may choose from the reading room, television lounge and the intimate Laird's Bar with its impressive range of malt whiskies. The picturesque village of Killin is just over two miles distant at the head of the loch. ♛ ♛ ♛ *Commended.*

BIRCHWOOD HOTEL,
2 East Moulin Road, Pitlochry,
Perthshire PH16 5DW

Tel: 0796 472477*
Fax: 0796 473951

Restricted licence; 17 bedrooms, all with private bathrooms; Historic interest; Children welcome, dogs by arrangement; Car park (25); Aberfeldy 14 miles; ££.

Set in the very heart of Scotland, Pitlochry is the ideal touring centre for many spectacular scenic, historic, sporting and entertainment pleasures. A fine Victorian building, Birchwood stands in 4 acres of lovely grounds just five minutes from the town centre. The spacious and light public and private rooms are attractively decorated and guest rooms have full en suite facilities, colour television, courtesy tray and central heating; all have delightful views over the gardens and Perthshire Hills. In such a tranquil and informal atmosphere, relaxation comes easily, aided in no small measure by the interesting table d'hôte and extensive à la carte menus available. A tip — a certain amount of control is advised if one is to appreciate the mouth-watering delights of the sweet trolley to the full! ♛ ♛ ♛ *Commended, AA and RAC**.*

CRAIGOWER HOTEL,
134 Atholl Road, Pitlochry,
Perthshire PH16 5AB

Tel and Fax: 0796 472590

Licensed; 26 bedrooms, all with private bathrooms; Children and pets welcome; Edinburgh 69 miles; Braemar 41; £.

Craigower is a family-run hotel in the centre of Pitlochry. We offer 26 comfortable en suite bedrooms, with television, hospitality tray, direct-dial telephone and hairdryer. Freshly prepared local produce is served in the restaurant. There is weekly entertainment in the hotel, and arrangements can be made for booking tickets at the local world-famous "Theatre in the Hills". Golf at one of the many local courses can be arranged, as can fishing and shooting. Open all year. **See also Colour Advertisement p.15.**

PORT-AN-EILEAN HOTEL,
Strathtummel, By Pitlochry,
Perthshire PH16 5RU

Tel: 0882 634233*

Fully licensed; 8 bedrooms, all with private bathrooms; Historic interest; Children and dogs welcome; Car park (20); Pitlochry 2 miles; ££.

Standing in 21 acres of grounds with far-reaching views of Loch Tummel and the mountains, this warm and welcoming hotel is beautifully situated at the beginning of the legendary 'Road to the Isles'. The atmosphere is entirely peaceful and guests may relax in true country house surroundings. Central heating is installed throughout and guest rooms are comfortably appointed, all having private bathrooms and tea and coffee-making facilities. Cuisine is of a high order, the menus being supported by an interesting wine list; children are well catered for and packed lunches are supplied on request. The hotel has a small cocktail bar and sun lounge and activities to be enjoyed nearby include fishing, sailing, shooting, golf and rambling. *Egon Ronay, Signpost Recommended.*

Ross-shire

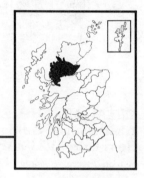

KINTAIL LODGE HOTEL,
Glenshiel, Kyle of Lochalsh,
Ross-shire IV40 8HL

Tel: 059-981 275*

Fax: 059-981 226

Fully licensed; 12 bedrooms, 10 with private bathrooms; Children welcome, dogs not allowed in public rooms; Car park (20); Kyle of Lochalsh 16 miles; £/££.

On the shores of picturesque Loch Duich, this former shooting lodge is surrounded by 4 acres of gardens and woodland and stands alongside the road that meanders from Inverness to the Isle of Skye. This is an area full of interest to historian and naturalist alike. For a relaxing holiday touring, walking, fishing or climbing, this fine, comfortably furnished hotel provides all the answers. Most of the bedrooms have private amenities and all have colour television, central heating and tea and coffee-making facilities. There are two well-stocked bars and excellent four-course dinners are served in a restaurant that overlooks the loch, local venison, salmon and shellfish figuring prominently on the menu. A laundry service is available and first-rate drying facilities exist. 🏵 🏵 🏵 *Commended.*

POOL HOUSE HOTEL,
Poolewe, By Achnasheen,
Ross-shire IV22 2LE

Tel: 044-586 272

Fax: 044-586 403

Fully licensed; 13 bedrooms, 11 with private bathrooms; Historic interest; Children welcome, pets by arrangement; Car park (40); Gairloch 4 miles; ££.

With a commanding position at the head of Loch Ewe, Pool House Hotel enjoys beautiful views across the bay to the famous Inverewe Gardens and the hills, coastline and islands that typify the grandeur of Wester Ross. There is a very cosy lounge where bar meals are served and a pleasant restaurant overlooking the bay. Here, visitors will soon feel relaxed and a favourite diversion is watching for salmon, seals and, sometimes, otters. In this area of outstanding natural beauty, one may walk, climb, swim in the lochs or in the indoor pool in the village, play golf and go boating at nearby Gairloch. The hotel is centrally heated and the attractive bedrooms are all equipped with colour television, radio and tea and coffee-making facilities; most have private amenities. 🏵 🏵 🏵 *Commended, RAC**.*

CREAG MOR HOTEL,
Charlestown, Gairloch,
Ross-shire IV21 2AH

Tel: 0445 2068

Fax: 0445 2044

Full hotel licence; 18 bedrooms, all with private bathrooms; Children and pets welcome; Car park (35); Poolewe 7 miles; ££.

Wining and dining to the highest standards is something taken for granted by visitors to this superbly furnished Highland hotel. The elegant Mackenzie Room specialises in salmon, trout, venison, prime beef and locally landed seafood, all complemented by a carefully chosen and extensive wine list. As a charming alternative to the restaurant, the Buttery is open all day for bar meals, coffee and snacks whilst, adjacent, is the convivial Bothan Bar, a popular meeting place which, in common with the cocktail bar, offers a selection of over 100 malt and blended whiskies. Known for its stunning decor, Creag Mor stands in its own extensive, landscaped grounds overlookinng Old Gairloch harbour and surrounded by the spectacular loch and mountain scenery of Wester Ross. From the imposing Gallery Lounge, bedecked with attractive water colours, there are splendid views of Skye and the Outer Isles. The popularity of this well-organised hotel is easy to understand for, kicking the dust of urban life from their heels, guests are assured of peace, comfort and every attention to their well-being as they relax. Recently refurbished bedrooms are colour co-ordinated throughout and provide en suite baths and showers, colour television, direct-dial telephone, tea and coffee-making facilities and 24-hour room service. There are several safe, sandy beaches nearby; also the world-famous Inverewe Gardens and opportunities for golf (9-hole), pony trekking, loch and sea fishing and watersports. 🌸 🌸 🌸 🌸 *Highly Commended, AA and RAC ***, Egon Ronay.*

Sutherland

BURGHFIELD HOUSE HOTEL,
Dornoch,
Sutherland IV25 3HN

Tel: 0862 810212*

Fax: 0862 810404

Fully licensed; 36 bedrooms, all with private bathrooms; Children and pets welcome; Car park (80); Bonar Bridge 13 miles; ££.

Only a few minutes from the famous Royal Dornoch Golf Course and miles of sandy beaches, the active diversions in the vicinity of this fine hotel will attract many visitors. Boats are also available for fishing in several lochs. However, those who have already experienced the much-acclaimed cuisine here will need no further inducement to return. The menus range from classical to Highland dishes using the best of local produce. Furnished to a high standard, this friendly and informal house has been efficiently run by the Currie family since 1946. Guest rooms are superbly equipped and there are two comfortable lounges, two cocktail bars, television and games rooms and plenty of space for children. ♛ ♛ ♛ ♛ *Commended.*

FOR THE MUTUAL GUIDANCE
OF GUEST AND HOST

Every year literally thousands of holidays, short-breaks and overnight stops are arranged through our guides, the vast majority without any problems at all. In a handful of cases, however, difficulties do arise about bookings, which often could have been prevented from the outset.

It is important to remember that when accommodation has been booked, both parties — guests and hosts — have entered into a form of contract. We hope that the following points will provide helpful guidance.

GUESTS: When enquiring about accommodation, be as precise as possible. Give exact dates, numbers in your party and the ages of any children. State the number and type of rooms wanted and also what catering you require — bed and breakfast, full board, etc. Make sure that the position about evening meals is clear — and about pets, reductions for children or any other special points.

Read our reviews carefully to ensure that the proprietors you are going to contact can supply what you want. Ask for a letter confirming all arrangements, if possible.

If you have to cancel, do so as soon as possible. Proprietors do have the right to retain deposits and under certain circumstances to charge for cancelled holidays if adequate notice is not given and they cannot re-let the accommodation.

HOSTS: Give details about your facilities and about any special conditions. Explain your deposit system clearly and arrangements for cancellations, charges, etc, and whether or not your terms include VAT.

If for any reason you are unable to fulfil an agreed booking without adequate notice, you may be under an obligation to arrange alternative suitable accommodation or to make some form of compensation.

While every effort is made to ensure accuracy, we regret that FHG Publications cannot accept responsibility for errors, omissions or misrepresentation in our entries or any consequences thereof. Prices in particular should be checked because we go to press early. We will follow up complaints but cannot act as arbiters or agents for either party.

Wigtownshire

CORSEMALZIE HOUSE HOTEL,
Port William, Newton Stewart,
Wigtownshire DG8 9RL

Tel: 098-886 254

Fully licensed; 14 bedrooms, all with private bathrooms; Historic interest; Children and pets welcome; Car park (35); Wigtown 6 miles; ££.

Set in the heart of picturesque countryside, this fine nineteenth century Scottish country mansion is surrounded by magnificent wooded grounds, and has been tastefully renovated to create a delightful and well appointed hotel, with a friendly, family atmosphere. The mild climate of this part of Scotland makes it ideal for a relaxing holiday at any time of year, and the wealth of leisure activities locally include walking, birdwatching, golf, fishing and pony trekking. The hotel is centrally heated throughout and the comfortable bedrooms all have private bath or shower, direct-dial telephone, remote-control colour television and tea-making facilities. A member of the "Taste of Scotland" scheme, the hotel enjoys a fine reputation for its imaginative cuisine. ♛♛♛ *Commended, AA and RAC***.*

ORDER NOW! *See Overleaf*

ONE FOR YOUR FRIEND 1993

FHG Publications have a large range of attractive holiday accommodation guides for all kinds of holiday opportunities throughout Britain. They also make useful gifts at any time of year. Our guides are available in most bookshops and larger newsagents but we will be happy to post you a copy direct if you have any difficulty. We will also post abroad but have to charge separately for post or freight.

The inclusive cost of posting and packing the guides to you or your friends in the UK is as follows:

Farm Holiday Guide ENGLAND, WALES and IRELAND
Board, Self-catering, Caravans/Camping, Activity Holidays. Over 400 pages. **£4.00**

Farm Holiday Guide SCOTLAND
All kinds of holiday accommodation. **£3.00**

SELF-CATERING & FURNISHED HOLIDAYS
Over 1000 addresses throughout for Self-catering and caravans in Britain. **£3.50**

BRITAIN'S BEST HOLIDAYS
A quick-reference general guide for all kinds of holidays. **£3.00**

The FHG Guide to CARAVAN & CAMPING HOLIDAYS
Caravans for hire, sites and holiday parks and centres. **£3.00**

BED AND BREAKFAST STOPS
Over 1000 friendly and comfortable overnight stops. Non-smoking, The Disabled and Special Diets Supplements. **£3.50**

CHILDREN WELCOME! FAMILY HOLIDAY GUIDE
Family holidays with details of amenities for children and babies. **£4.00**

Recommended SHORT BREAK HOLIDAYS IN BRITAIN
'Approved' accommodation for quality bargain breaks. Introduced by John Carter. **£4.00**

Recommended COUNTRY HOTELS OF BRITAIN
Including Country Houses, for the discriminating. **£4.00**

Recommended WAYSIDE INNS OF BRITAIN
Pubs, Inns and small hotels. **£4.00**

THE GOLF GUIDE Where to Play and Where to Stay
Over 2000 golf courses in Britain with convenient accommodation. Endorsed by the PGA. Holiday Golf in France, Portugal and Majorca. **£8.50**

PETS WELCOME!
The unique guide for holidays for pet owners and their pets. **£4.00**

BED AND BREAKFAST IN BRITAIN
Over 1000 choices for touring and holidays throughout Britain. Airports and Ferries Supplement. **£3.00**

THE FRENCH FARM AND VILLAGE HOLIDAY GUIDE
The official guide to self-catering holidays in the 'Gîtes de France'. **£8.50**

Tick your choice and send your order and payment to FHG PUBLICATIONS, ABBEY MILL BUSINESS CENTRE, SEEDHILL, PAISLEY PA1 1TJ (TEL: 041-887 0428. FAX: 041-889 7204). **Deduct** 10% for 2/3 titles or copies; 20% for 4 or more.

Send to: NAME ....

ADDRESS ....

....

.... POST CODE ....

I enclose Cheque/Postal Order for £ ....

SIGNATURE .... DATE ....

144

MAP
SECTION

The following seven pages of maps indicate the main
cities, towns and holiday centres of Britain. Space
obviously does not permit every location featured in
this book to be included but the approximate position
may be ascertained by using the distance indications
quoted and the scale bars on the maps.

Map 1

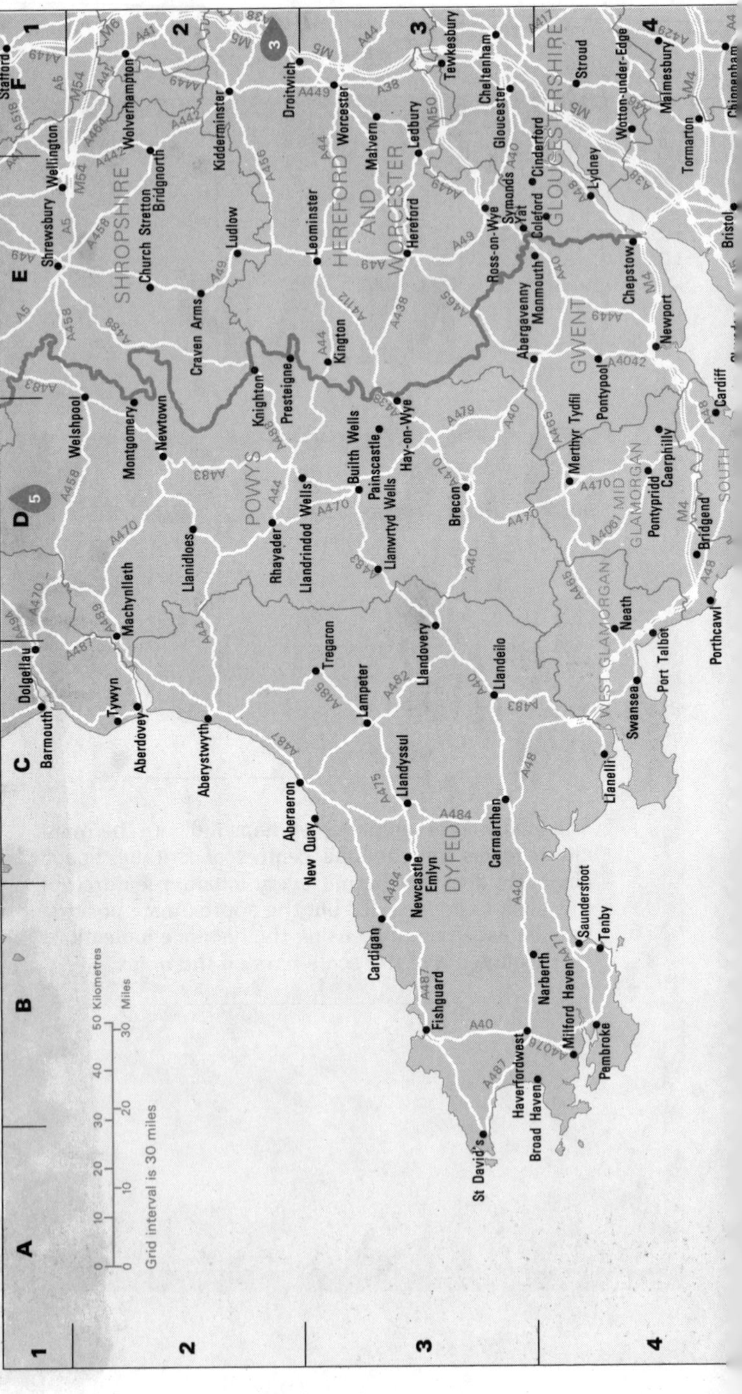

A
B
C
D
E
F
1
2
3
4
Stafford
Wellington
Wolverhampton
Shrewsbury
Church Stretton
Bridgnorth
Kidderminster
Droitwich
Worcester
Ludlow
Leominster
Malvern
Ledbury
Tewkesbury
Cheltenham
Gloucester
Hereford
Ross-on-Wye
Symonds Yat
Cinderford
Coleford
Stroud
Lydney
Wotton-under-Edge
Malmesbury
Tormarton
Bristol
Chepstow
Monmouth
Abergavenny
Newport
Cardiff
Pontypool
Caerphilly
Merthyr Tydfil
Pontypridd
Bridgend
Porthcawl
Neath
Port Talbot
Swansea
Llanelli
Craven Arms
Kington
Presteigne
Knighton
Welshpool
Montgomery
Newtown
Builth Wells
Painscastle
Hay-on-Wye
Llandrindod Wells
Llanwrtyd Wells
Brecon
Rhayader
Llanidloes
Machynlleth
Dolgellau
Barmouth
Tywyn
Aberdovey
Aberystwyth
Tregaron
Lampeter
Llandovery
Llandeilo
Aberaeron
New Quay
Llandyssul
Newcastle Emlyn
Cardigan
Carmarthen
Saundersfoot
Tenby
Narberth
Fishguard
Haverfordwest
Milford Haven
Pembroke
Broad Haven
St David's
SHROPSHIRE
HEREFORD AND WORCESTER
GLOUCESTERSHIRE
GWENT
POWYS
MID GLAMORGAN
SOUTH
WEST GLAMORGAN
DYFED
0 10 20 30 40 50 Kilometres
0 10 20 30 Miles
Grid interval is 30 miles

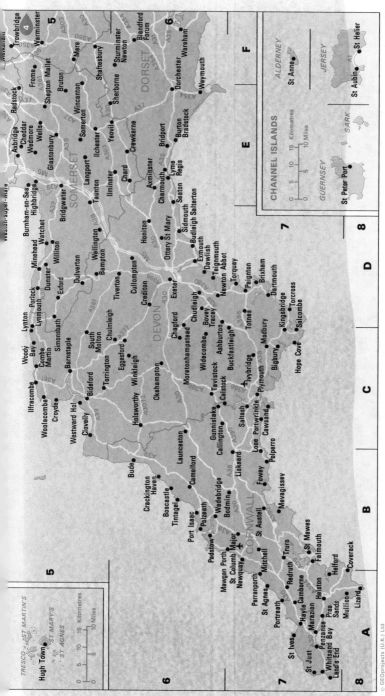

Map 2

Map 3

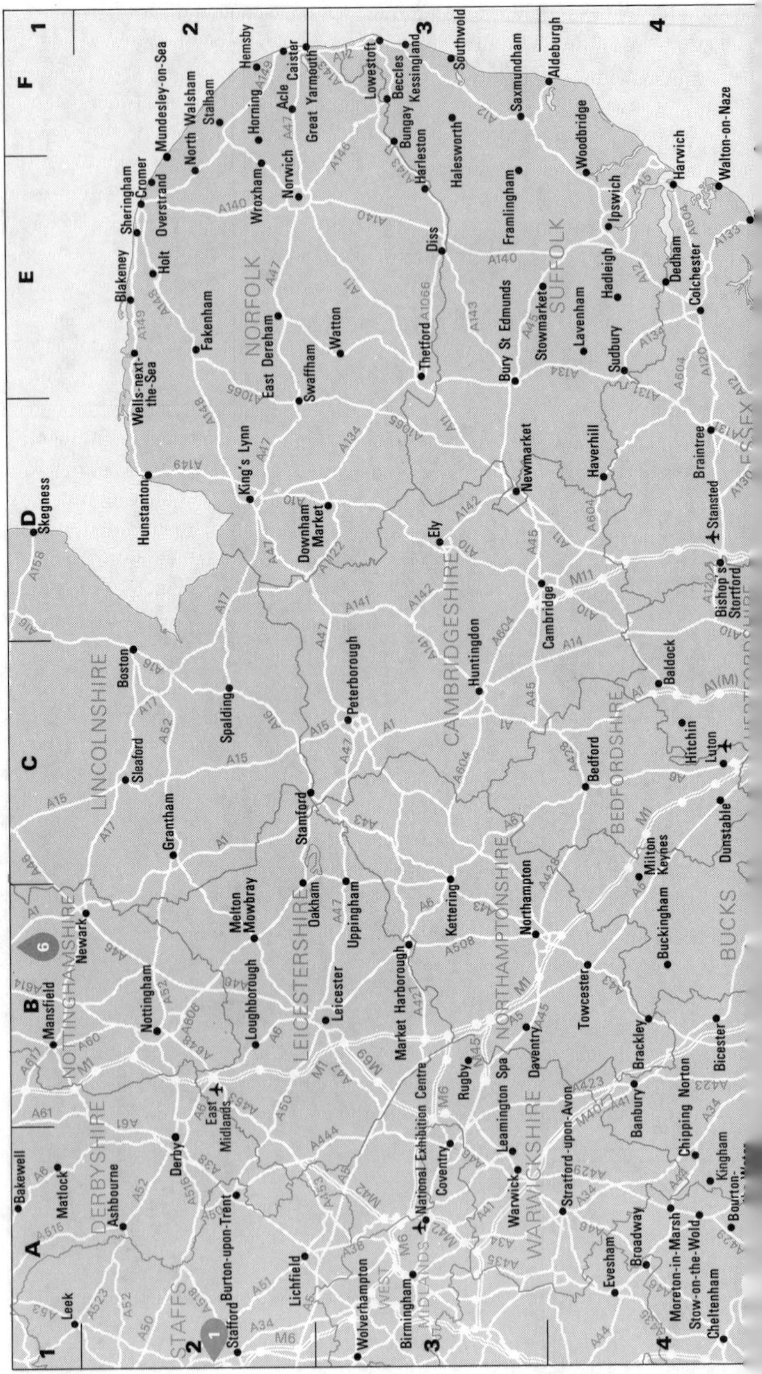

A
B
C
D
E
F
1
2
3
4
LINCOLNSHIRE
NOTTINGHAMSHIRE
DERBYSHIRE
STAFFS
LEICESTERSHIRE
NORTHAMPTONSHIRE
WARWICKSHIRE
WEST MIDLANDS
CAMBRIDGESHIRE
BEDFORDSHIRE
BUCKS
NORFOLK
SUFFOLK
ESSEX
Skegness
Hunstanton
Wells-next-the-Sea
Blakeney
Sheringham
Cromer
Overstrand
Mundesley-on-Sea
North Walsham
Stalham
Hemsby
Horning
Wroxham
Holt
Fakenham
East Dereham
Swaffham
Watton
King's Lynn
Downham Market
Norwich
Acle
Caister
Great Yarmouth
Lowestoft
Beccles
Kessingland
Bungay
Harleston
Southwold
Halesworth
Saxmundham
Aldeburgh
Framlingham
Woodbridge
Ipswich
Harwich
Walton-on-Naze
Diss
Thetford
Bury St Edmunds
Stowmarket
Lavenham
Hadleigh
Sudbury
Dedham
Colchester
Newmarket
Haverhill
Braintree
Stansted
Bishop's Stortford
Ely
Cambridge
Huntingdon
Peterborough
Baldock
Hitchin
Luton
Bedford
Dunstable
Milton Keynes
Boston
Spalding
Sleaford
Grantham
Stamford
Melton Mowbray
Oakham
Uppingham
Kettering
Northampton
Newark
Mansfield
Nottingham
Loughborough
Leicester
Market Harborough
Towcester
Buckingham
Daventry
Rugby
Leamington Spa
Warwick
Coventry
National Exhibition Centre
Brackley
Bicester
Banbury
Chipping Norton
Kingham
Bourton-
Stratford-upon-Avon
Evesham
Broadway
Moreton-in-Marsh
Stow-on-the-Wold
Cheltenham
Birmingham
Wolverhampton
Lichfield
Stafford
Burton-upon-Trent
East Midlands
Derby
Ashbourne
Matlock
Bakewell
Leek

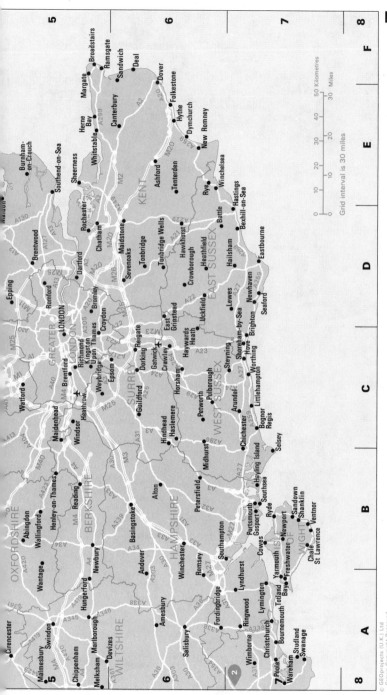

Map 4

Map 5

Map 6

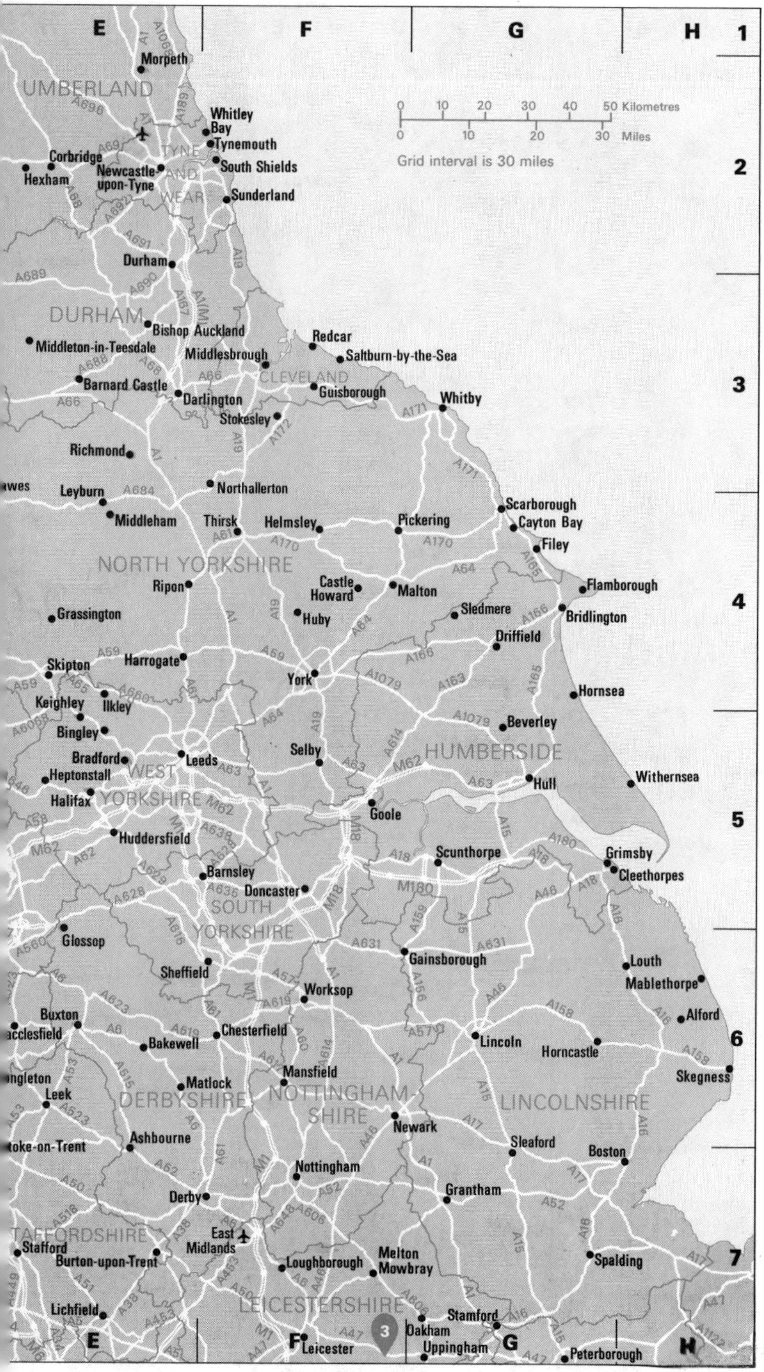

Grid interval is 30 miles

| | 0 | 10 | 20 | 30 | 40 | 50 Kilometres |
| | 0 | | 10 | 20 | | 30 Miles |

Morpeth

NORTHUMBERLAND

Whitley Bay
Tynemouth
South Shields
Sunderland

Corbridge
Newcastle upon-Tyne
TYNE AND WEAR

Hexham

Durham

DURHAM

Bishop Auckland

Middleton-in-Teesdale
Redcar
Middlesbrough
Saltburn-by-the-Sea
CLEVELAND

Barnard Castle
Darlington
Guisborough
Whitby

Stokesley

Richmond

Hawes
Leyburn
Northallerton

Middleham
Thirsk
Helmsley
Pickering
Scarborough
Cayton Bay
Filey

NORTH YORKSHIRE

Ripon
Castle Howard
Malton
Flamborough

Grassington
Huby
Sledmere
Bridlington

Driffield

Skipton
Harrogate
York
Hornsea

Keighley
Ilkley
Selby
Beverley

Bingley
Leeds
HUMBERSIDE

Bradford
Hull
Withernsea

Heptonstall
Goole

Halifax
WEST YORKSHIRE

Huddersfield
Scunthorpe
Grimsby
Cleethorpes

Barnsley
Doncaster

Glossop
SOUTH YORKSHIRE
Gainsborough
Louth
Mablethorpe

Sheffield
Worksop

Buxton
Chesterfield
Lincoln
Horncastle
Alford

Macclesfield
Bakewell
Skegness

Congleton
Matlock
Mansfield
LINCOLNSHIRE

Leek
DERBYSHIRE
NOTTINGHAM-SHIRE
Newark
Sleaford
Boston

Stoke-on-Trent
Ashbourne

Derby
Nottingham
Grantham

STAFFORDSHIRE
East Midlands

Stafford
Loughborough
Melton Mowbray
Spalding

Burton-upon-Trent

Lichfield
LEICESTERSHIRE
Stamford

Leicester
Oakham
Uppingham
Peterborough